Project Procurement
A Real-World Guide for Procurement Skills

Ajay Bhargove, C.Eng, MIE, PMP

Library of Congress Cataloging-in-Publication Data

Names: Bhargove, Ajay, author.
Title: Project procurement : a real-world guide for procurement skills / Ajay
  Bhargove, C.Eng, MIE, PMP.
Description: Newtown Square, Pennsylvania : Project Management Institute,
  Inc., [2018] | Includes bibliographical references and index.
Identifiers: LCCN 2017053649 (print) | LCCN 2017055622 (ebook) | ISBN
  9781628254693 (ePUB) | ISBN 9781628254709 (kindle) | ISBN 9781628254716 (
  Web PDF) | ISBN 9781628254686 (pbk. : alk. paper)
Subjects: LCSH: Project management. | Purchasing. | Industrial procurement.
Classification: LCC HD69.P75 (ebook) | LCC HD69.P75 B49995 2018 (print) | DDC
  658.7—dc23
LC record available at https://lccn.loc.gov/2017053649

ISBN: 978-1-62825-468-6

Published by: Project Management Institute, Inc.
            14 Campus Boulevard
            Newtown Square, Pennsylvania 19073-3299 USA
            Phone: +1 610-356-4600
            Fax: +1 610-482-9971
            Email: customercare@pmi.org
            Internet: PMI.org

To inquire about discounts for resale or educational purposes, please contact the PMI Book
Service Center.

            PMI Book Service Center
            P.O. Box 932683, Atlanta, GA 31193-2683 USA
            Phone: +1 866-276-4764 (within the U.S. or Canada) or
            + 1 770-280-4129 (globally)
            Fax: + 1 770-280-4113
            Email: info@bookorders.pmi.org

Table of Contents

Acknowledgments

I am grateful to my enthusiastic son, Aarav Bhargava, and my lovely daughter, Ahana Bhargava, for giving me the time needed to write this book. It was a great effort. I am also grateful to my mother, Dr. Urmila Devi, who has been an unceasing source of inspiration. When my mind grows resistant to trying something new, I can always count on my elder brother, Vijay, whose positive energy always keeps me going.

Thanks also go to the entire team of people supporting me in accomplishing this milestone—a journey that I began two years ago. I do not want to write a book for academics, but would like to share the complete practical experience I have attained over the years.

My next big thanks go to my wife, Vandana, for managing all her time with our kids when I was not able to and also for lending her time to editing this book. It was a pain and pleasure to go through the first complete edit. Her performance has been excellent throughout this process, and without her, producing this book would not have been possible.

I would be remiss if I did not acknowledge my past and present friends who kept me motivated throughout the years of preparation needed to accomplish this dream project.

CHAPTER 1

Introduction

If you are a beginner in supply chain management or buying, then you will find this chapter an important building block for understanding the rest of the chapters of this book; experienced procurement professionals will find this chapter to be a refresher of knowledge previously gained.

This chapter covers the following topics:

- Definitions
- Project Stages
- Procurement Life Cycle and Importance in Project Management
- Types of Procurement
- Budgets and Reserves

1.1 Definitions

It is important to begin with an understanding of the terms related to buying. Reading these terms carefully will go a long way in any attempt at making a career in buying, from junior buyer up to supply chain head of organizations, so let us have a look at some of these important definitions.

1.1.1 Purchase Requisitions

Purchase requisitions are formal requests raised by the department that is requesting the supply chain department to outsource goods and/or services.

1.1.2 Procurement

Procurement is an all-inclusive function that describes the activities and processes used to acquire goods and services. Importantly, and distinct from *purchasing*, procurement includes the activities involved in establishing fundamental requirements; sourcing activities, such as market research and vendor evaluation; and negotiation of contracts. In short, purchasing is a subset of procurement functions.

1.1.3 Project Procurement

A project-specific procurement function is referred to as project procurement. In the past, procurement was a decentralized function because it was understood as a support function rather than a specialized job. With the increase of competition and organizational complexity, project procurement was made a centralized function, requiring experts to deal with ever-changing conditions and keep track of the market at all times. However, this was also not very helpful, as organizations buying everything with the same standard specifications (that do not conform to client or end customer requirements) resulted in organizations becoming less cost beneficial. As organizations started losing orders, the need for setting up a project procurement department was felt; however, experts added this function based on particular project requirements rather than for the purposes of providing a high-quality end product.

1.1.4 Purchasing

The term *purchasing* refers to the process of ordering and receiving goods and services. It is a subset of the procurement process, as explained above. Generally, purchasing refers to the process involved in ordering goods such as the request, approval, or creation of a purchase order (PO) record, and the receiving of goods. Therefore, in simple words, purchasing is a subset of procurement and is part of procurement functions.

1.1.5 Auction

An auction is a sort of public bidding system, where the bids can be submitted repeatedly any number of times until a decided end time—or earlier if somebody has won the deal.

1.1.6 E-Auction

An electronic way of negotiating a contract or an agreement is known as an e-auction. E-auctions can be conducted in a number of formats, such as a reverse auction, Dutch auction, English auction, and so forth. It is important to understand the basis of choosing a particular type of e-auction method. Although we will learn more about this in Chapter 6, popular electronic auctions are introduced and briefly described as follows.

- **Dutch auction**

    A Dutch auction is a method of reducing prices until a buyer is found. This type of auction starts with the highest possible price at which the selling organization wants to sell their goods and/or services, and in the case that no buyer is ready to accept the selling organization price, then the selling organization reduces the price. This is an iterative process, as the seller keeps on reducing the selling price until the buyer accepts the offered selling price. Dutch auctions are not popular with project organizations, as project organizations buy material based on competition among different sellers.

- **English auction**

  An English auction is a type of forward auction, where the seller sets the reserve price and then the price is incremented until the highest price is received. This is a traditional method of auction. For example, when somebody wants to sell a painting with the lowest price set at US$1 million and the price is increased by US$200,000 with every new bid. In such an auction, the bidder with the highest price gets the painting.

- **Reverse auction**

  A reverse auction is way of agreeing on a contract, where competing suppliers keep on reducing the prices at which they are ready to provide the goods and/or services to the buyer. The lowest bidding supplier wins the contract.

1.1.7 Logistics

This term was first used by the military for all the activities of armed-force units in support of war units, including transport, supply, communications, medical aid, and personnel. In the business context, this is used for handling the complete operation, from picking up the material from the agreed-upon place through the time period of the material being stored at the required destinations.

1.2 Project Stages

It is ideal for readers to understand the various project stages and the role to be played by the procurement team during each stage. Procurement has an important role to play within the business unit. Figure 1.1 illustrates that procurement can support the tendering team in preparing an offer. Also, once the offer is submitted by the sales team to the customer, the customer can request

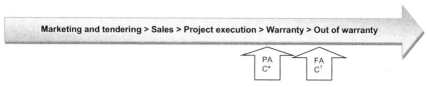

*PAC : Provisional acceptance
[1]FAC : Final acceptance

Figure 1.1: Project stages.

further discounts; procurement/tendering can rework the costing for revision of the offer. During execution, procurement has an active role to play and has to support the project management team to ensure the business unit has set up a project margin.

Most organizations make the mistake of acknowledging the role of procurement during the tendering stage, which leads to less business and higher risks during execution.

1.2.1 Marketing and Tendering

Marketing and tendering is an important phase; normally both are understood to be the same thing, but they are, in fact, entirely different. Marketing is about marketing an organization's products and searching for potential customers. Once the potential customers start finding interest in an organization's products, the sales and tendering people pitch in. Sales teams mark a particular customer as an opportunity, whereas tendering teams start working on the estimates, costs, and prices to be offered to the customer.

1.2.2 Sales

The sales team works based on the leads generated by the marketing team, and once agreeing on the bid/no bid, they request tendering to prepare the offer based on the customer's requirements. The sales team meets with the customer several times before the customer makes a decision to go with the supplying organizations for the customer's project requirements of goods and/or services.

1.2.3 Project Execution

Once the sales team has secured the project order from the customer, it hands the project order over to the project execution team during the formal project kick-off meeting. These kick-off meetings are important since they define the deliverables in detail as well as other critical factors. After the project kick-off meeting, the contracting organization starts working on a detailed project schedule and project plan. This is the phase where project execution delivers what was agreed upon with the customer, whether this includes products, services, or both. If the customer is satisfied with what they have appointed the organization to provide, they sign the provisional acceptance/project handover formally. This is an important stage after which the warranty period starts, and will be discussed below.

1.2.4 Warranty

The customer has taken over the project delivered by the contracting organization by signing the project handover or provisional acceptance of works. Because every product has a life, and based on the returns on investment, if anything goes wrong, the contracting organization has to repair any defects or replace the products as agreed upon under the contract with the customer. Normally, the contracting organization has a clear idea about their own product reliability and shelf life, so they have nothing to lose by agreeing to warranty terms. In spite of product life, the contracting organization keeps a 3% to 5% budget for any uncertainties. After successful completion of the warranty phase, contracting organizations are not bound to make any rectification, even if any condition arises. However, the customer can ask the organization to make corrections at additional costs and expenses, which is a normal practice across the globe until or unless the products or services become obsolete.

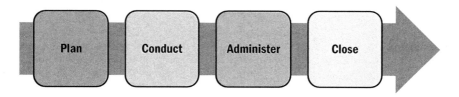

Figure 1.2: Project procurement life cycle.

1.3 Procurement Life Cycle

Understanding the procurement life cycle can change the way you do it. Procurement generally starts with planning what to buy, where to buy, when to buy, and how much to buy, and then concludes with closing the contract.

Figure 1.2 shows that before transforming the requirements into finished products, services, or results, there are several steps to be taken that may fall into one of the illustrated areas.

1.3.1 Plan Procurement

This is about the planning of procurement, which covers what to buy, when to buy, how and how much to buy, and what contract type to be used.

1.3.2 Conduct Procurement

Conduct procurement is about finalizing the order award. This covers the steps involved in making requests for quotes, conducting bidder's conferences and strategic negotiations, and awarding the contract.

1.3.3 Administer Procurement

This is where the contract is being administered against the contract requirements, and only the appropriate changes to the contract order are being discussed for further approval from the change control board or approval committee.

1.3.4 Close Procurement

This is the final phase in the procurement—the time to formally close the order and settle all possible claims. However, it should be noted that even if there are unsettled claims, the phase needs to be completed.

1.4 Sector-Based Procurement

Doing procurement can be defined in many ways, which vary from organization to organization, and country to country. We should keep our focus on the ways in which it is being handled generally. Sector-based procurement can be divided broadly into two categories, government sector and private sector.

1.4.1 Government Sector

Government sector utilities and public-private partnership companies must follow the guidelines laid down by the respective regulators (if appointed). Otherwise, all cases need to follow the guidelines of a central vigilance commission, or any other circulars or amendments being issued by the competent authority.

1.4.2 Private Sector

The private sector is highly dependent on the type of sector and the organization's internal policies. In the case of regional organizations or small entities, you may not even find any policies; such organizations follow the instructions of the entity's head in all cases. However, in the case of multinational companies, there are usually established processes and guidelines inherited from their headquarters with alignment to local and international rules and regulations.

1.5 Budgets and Reserves

If you are working for an organization that is more dependent on external projects, or projects coming from outside customers or clients, then knowledge of the following types of budgets is critical.

Every organization during the sales phase keeps some documentation on perceived risks and profits. So, when one organization makes an offer to another organization, it is not only the cost of the raw material plus the profit margin, it is also dependent on the style of the organization to bid for external customers. Despite the fact that different organizations can have different ways of arriving at project costs, they will keep following types of reserves in addition to other projects costs to meet any unforeseen costs, which otherwise impact the complete profit margin.

1.5.1 Management Reserves

The management reserves are generally the reserves that every organization keeps based on future uncertainties from any of its projects or from some external factor(s). The important point to remember is that management reserves are not in the hands of the project manager, and in case of project cost overruns, the project manager has to request top management to release additional budget funds from this reserve. Whether to continue the project with such a loss or just terminate it is, again, solely the decision of top management. These may be understood as "known cost provisions for unknown risks."

1.5.2 Contingency Reserves

Every project should have a contingency reserve, which should be decided on in the very initial stages, preferably while bidding, but not later than accepting the order from the external customer. This is also known as "provisions created for the known risks," which if they pop up, will have to be mitigated with additional costs. In other words, we may say that these are the known cost provisions for known risks.

CHAPTER 2

Supplier Management

Every one of us might be wondering why companies have to spend a lot of resources, including time, money, and manpower, in supplier management activities such as supplier qualification, supplier performance evaluation, supplier development, and phaseout decisions. There's only one answer to this question, which follows:

Supplier management is less costly than the risk of project failure. If suppliers are not able to deliver what they were contracted for, then contracting organizations lose a lot of money implementing risk purchase, and disaster comes as a project loss.

2.1 Definitions

The following terms will help in understanding complete supplier management activities:

- **Supplier**
- **Supplier Qualification**
- **Supplier Evaluation**
- **Supplier Development**
- **Supplier Phaseout**

2.2 Supplier Management Life Cycle

Figure 2.1 depicts the complete life cycle of supplier management, which starts from supplier identification. Once the supplier is selected, they will be qualified and subsequently evaluated during the complete life cycle phases of the project, which are, in general, classified as pre-award, execution, and warranty phase (closing). Once the supplier has been evaluated for all the phases of the project life cycle, they can be classified as the preferred supplier, or categorized based on the organization's methodology of classifying suppliers.

Also clear from the life cycle of supplier management (Figure 2.1), is that once the supplier has been classified, then some of the suppliers may be selected as a non-useful supplier for the organization's future project or business.

We use the word non-useful, as this may be based on bad experiences with the supplier, or may be because of the organization's decision not to take specific projects in the future.

To understand this, let's review an example:

Suppose Organization A is involved in building nuclear power plants and has decided to come out of this business for internal reasons, such as loss in previous projects, or external factors like government regulations. Obviously, Organization A would not request the same set of suppliers in the future, were this

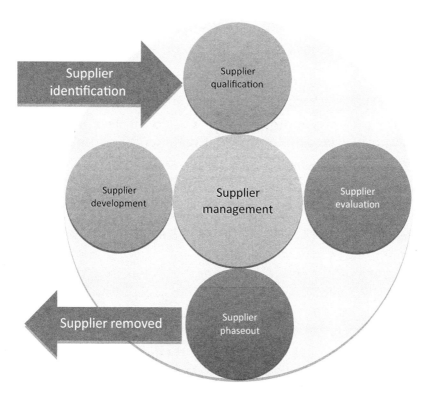

Figure 2.1:   Supplier management turbo.

organization to begin executing, for example, information technology projects instead.

Based on the supplier's successful evaluation results, the organization may decide to develop a particular supplier for future projects and may decide to support the supplier by suggesting any modifications that may be in the production line—or by suggesting more efficient ways to produce the end product with lesser costs. This is an area that may be said to be part of continuous improvement in customer-supplier relationships.

2.2.1 Supplier Selection and Qualification

The supplier selection process is very important prior to making any purchase decision; certainly, you don't want to send out a request for proposal to the whole world. There would be obvious additional costs, time, and effort required to evaluate the offers received from the suppliers, as today's world is competitive and demands that "just the right supplier" be considered, instead of considering everyone as an approved supplier.

We, as a buying organization, should be clear about whom we want to consider for our requirements. While selecting the supplier, the organization may also decide the criteria for supplier evaluations up front, and with concerned departments like engineering, quality assurance and quality control, project procurement, and project management. Supplier qualification is very important to perform and advance, along with supplier selection, as it would lead to less time getting approval from management, the end customer, or the project owner—and later, nobody will question the purchase proposal prepared by the purchase department.

Sometimes the end customer would like to be involved in the process of selecting the vendor for their project. The end customer providing the list of approved suppliers to the contracting organization can achieve this, or the client may decide to take on the decision during the order award if the awarded supplier is different from the approved supplier list for the project. The buying organization must look into the approved supplier list, if provided, to avoid supplier acceptance discussions later with the end client. By providing an approved supplier list for the project, the client is not promoting any particular supplier, but is trying to use this supplier list as a filter to avoid the contracting organization supplying it with inferior materials or products.

Supplier evaluation criteria are based on two factors: lessons learned from past projects and future forecasting for the supplier. Therefore, criteria may be decided based on earlier projects, including claims made by the supplier during the execution of past projects; any costs incurred on behalf of the supplier because of their own failure to execute the work, the risk purchase, or purchase on behalf of the supplier; any in delivering the material by the supplier at the desired location (i.e., a logistics failure);

any cost for the perceived risk in going with the particular supplier; and any additional expediting costs if we select a particular supplier. In other words, evaluation criteria will help in reducing the evaluation time and also provide the complete picture while selecting one supplier over another. Supplier selection is part of supplier qualification, and once the supplier is qualified, then the criteria for supplier evaluation can be decided. Therefore, the organization may have both of the above (supplier selection and supplier evaluation) as different processes, or they can be done simultaneously.

If we do not visit the supplier's works while qualifying them, we would never know the kind of risk-prone areas that could have the potential for compliance and delivery delays.

2.2.2 Supplier Evaluation

Once the supplier is selected and has been considered for outsourcing, along with some of the work or work packages for a specific project, then the supplier needs to be continuously evaluated for conforming to the requirements, and the evaluation should be used to compare the supplier performance against the project-specific requirements, including engineering, procurement, logistics, and quality. Systematic supplier evaluation, as feedback on the supplier's performance, forms the basis for efficient supplier development for future projects and also helps to improve the supplier's relationship with the customer and the supplier's performance. Supplier evaluation results will become the input to the supplier development and phasing out the non-performing suppliers for future business.

An argument for evaluating supplier performance needs to be made. After all, a lot of resources, including time, have already been spent on the supplier evaluation process.

When I started my career as a buyer, I was of the opinion that it is important to have a good supplier. Everybody needs the best people doing the job, irrespective of the job requirements. Ask engineering colleagues: They only want to evaluate the supplier so that they can report the supplier behavior and performance during the project, and in the future, will know who the good supplier is and who best supplier is. However, from the engineering point of view, the preference is to have the suppliers who follow the instructions of the engineering department and provide support beyond the contract if required. The point is that everybody uses their own yardstick to measure supplier performance. It is better to integrate all the concerned people and let them evaluate the supplier performance; this may include procurement, logistics, engineering, quality, and so on.

2.2.3 Supplier Classification

Once the supplier evaluation is complete, you have the results of evaluations, and you know which supplier has performed as per your expectations and which has failed to meet the requirements. Now you can classify them as poor, average, good, and excellent—or whatever category you want to assign.

There will likely be a supplier who you don't want to consider for future business, and there can be some who you want to further improve. There may be another set of suppliers who have excellent performance.

2.2.4 Supplier Phaseout

The supplier phaseout decision is generally made by the customer based on supplier evaluation results and internal business management decisions. The phasing out decision should not be compared with blacklisting the supplier, as phaseout may happen because the closure of a particular sector of the organization, so the organization is simply not in need of the supplier in the future.

This decision is generally a strategic call and it should be communicated to the supplier even if an organization decides to phase out a supplier because of bad performance. It is not always a good option to phase out a supplier, especially for a patented item or a supplier with the monopoly in the market for a particular item.

2.2.5 Supplier Development

Every organization would like to further develop the suppliers who are top performers and have helped the customer's organization in meeting their goals. Supplier development comes with an increase in spending to award more work to a particular supplier, for local as well as global projects. Supplier development is required, since every organization needs quality suppliers who will be further used in tendering, costing, and estimation for future projects. Initially, supplier development has to be on a trial basis if it is based on increased area of work, such as using the supplier for new work for which they have not yet been evaluated.

2.3 Cost of Quality

Cost of quality is important to understand in getting the answers to the question: Why perform supplier management activities?

Cost of quality includes all costs incurred over the life of the product by investing for prevention of non-conformance costs.

Therefore, cost of quality can be defined as every sum that is spent to meet quality requirements, including prevention costs, appraisal costs, and cost of non-conformance (if any).

Therefore:

Cost of Quality = Prevention Costs + Appraisal Costs + Non-Conformance Costs

2.3.1 Cost of Conformance

Cost of conformance can be understood as the cost to avoid failures in order to meet customer requirements. This can include various costs, as detailed in Figure 2.2, like the cost for training

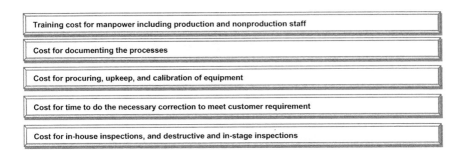

Figure 2.2:   Cost of conformance.

the production staff, documentation, equipment, and timely calibrations as well as destructive testing of equipment. These costs are incurred by the supplier to comply with requirements, and are lower as compared to costs of non-conformance (see Figure 2.3).

The cost of conformance comprises two types of costs, defined as follows:

- **Prevention costs**

  These costs involve employee training, documenting processes, and procurement of equipment for manufacturing what is required.

- **Appraisal costs**

  These costs involve inspection, destructive testing, and so forth.

Defect correction costs found by customer during inspection of material

Figure 2.3:   Cost of non-conformance.

2.3.2. Cost of Non-Conformance

Costs of non-conformance are the costs required because of an organization's failure to comply with project requirements.

- **Internal failure costs**

  These are costs that are found by the manufacturer and are incurred because of reworking to comply with customer requirements and/or are due to the complete scrapping of the products under manufacturing. If you are an experienced buyer, you may have heard from the supplier that delivery is getting delayed because of a quality issue at the supplier's end.

- **External failure costs**

  These costs appear because of defects found by the customer; and normally, such costs are very high. These can be liabilities, warranty costs, and so on.

Therefore, the cost of non-conformance can be due to following factors, as detailed in Figure 2.3.

CHAPTER **3**

Bidding and Methods

This chapter discusses methods for getting information from internal or external organizations.

3.1 Definitions

- **Request for quotation**

  A request for quotation (RFQ) is a standard business process inviting suppliers into a bidding process to bid on specific products or services. RFQ generally means the same thing as invitation for bid (IFB). An RFQ typically involves more than the price per item.

- **Request for information**

  A request for information (RFI) is a standard business process for collecting written information about the capabilities of various suppliers. Normally, it follows a format that can be used for comparative purposes.

- **Request for proposal**

  A request for proposal (RFP) is a solicitation to potential suppliers to submit business proposals, often made through a bidding process, by an agency or company interested in procurement of a commodity, service, or valuable asset.

3.2 Methods for Inviting Information and/or Offers

There can be many ways of doing this particular activity, which can generally be classified in the following ways:

3.2.1 Manual

This method offers information (or information is invited) in hard copies only. This system of inviting offers is popular with government entities, where bidders have to buy the RFQ/RFI from the government office, and thereafter, based on the received RFQ/RFI, the interested bidders can submit the offer in hard copies to the organization's procurement office. These days, even government entities are converting to electronic methods of inviting offers or information.

3.2.2 Electronic

This method of inviting offers and/or information is utilized by private organizations, where speed and accuracy matter more than transparency, since public money is not involved in private organizations. This system of inviting offers and/or information has gained new heights in the last decade, as several online tools and software are developed with good levels of data security.

3.3 Types of Bidding

When we say bidding, it means the method in which we can submit the offer against any proposal for offer or for information. This really depends on the type of organization and how the organization sees a particular end product. For one organization, the end product may be highly complex, whereas for other organizations, it may be a simple end product with less complexity.

3.3.1 Single-Part Bidding

Single-part bidding is a way to invite all the details into a single techno-commercial offer, which may involve a technical offer as well as a commercial offer. This kind of bidding is practiced to reduce the procurement cycle time and is generally used for requirements with fewer technicalities.

3.3.2 Two-Part Bidding

In two-part bidding systems, bids are invited in two parts; the first part comprises the techno-commercial, and the second part consists of the price bid. In such a system, the first techno-commercial offer is evaluated and based on qualified bidders; price bids are opened in public.

3.4 Important Facts for Inviting Information and/or Offers

3.4.1 Use Appropriate Size RFQ

The buyer needs to decide how clearly, they can communicate the requirement to suppliers. The buying organization has a template for communicating the requirements, so it becomes crucial to use the correct RFQ template. On projects, requirements may vary from a simple iron bar to high-complexity turbines; hence, the template for the RFQ is selected appropriately. Obviously, the RFQ template for a steam turbine would be detailed, as compared to iron bar requirements. If the buyer fails to use the appropriate template, it will lead to increased costs based on uncertain risk buffers considered by the seller in their offer. The appropriate size of the RFQ will help in getting the quotation faster, and results in less time spent on clarifying the requirements during clarification meetings with the supplier.

3.4.2 Use Your Own RFQ Template and Content

It is not recommended that the buyer use the RFQ template with the content as provided by the supplier in earlier site meetings or in the office. The path to making that particular supplier a "sole supplier," may bring many risks, which will lead to fewer advantages for the buying organization, as no other alternative will be available. By doing this, the buyer would be on their way to float the specifications that are completely irrelevant to them, but serve to exclude the competition.

3.4.3 Use an RFI Before an RFQ If It Makes Sense to Do so

If one supplier is your main source of market information, you can first issue a request for information (RFI) to learn more about the market. Selling organizations are very quick to list copious specifications in an RFQ.

The best way to approach the market is to identify a problem or pain that you have and let experts in that particular market tell you how they would resolve it.

3.4.4 Engagement with Supplier Prior to RFQ

If the first time a supplier hears of a sales opportunity is when they receive an RFQ, this works to the buyer's disadvantage, as suppliers are likely to predict a small chance of winning and will not invest their best effort into making a response to the RFQ, if they respond at all. You really are aided by picking up the telephone and calling a supplier, introducing yourself, explaining what you're looking for, and building a long-term relationship with the supplier. This should, and must, be done prior to issuance of an RFQ.

3.4.5 Avoid Checklists in the RFQ

When buying organizations are sourcing, they want to try out the maximum supplier base, which may include the set of candidates from a pool of qualified suppliers and may also include prospective suppliers. Many of these offers can provide lower pricing and a higher quality of service. I have observed that putting checklists involving "yes" or "no" questions does the opposite, and are often used to put a check on suppliers, which does not fit with the customer requirements. This approach will ease the supplier quotation evaluation process, but it creates a wall when submitting the quotation to suppliers who may be able to meet the functional requirements but not the standard questionnaire requirements. Hence, either have your questionnaire revised based on your supplier base or avoid using a standard questionnaire.

3.4.6 Take Appropriate Time for Making an RFQ

While preparing the RFQ, it is important for the buyer to spend appropriate time on its preparation. Clauses like offer validity, warranty terms, and payment terms based on milestones or order type should be revisited before releasing the RFQ.

3.4.7 Participation Fee

In a disturbing observation, some organizations have been involved in situations where they have asked suppliers to pay to participate in the organization's RFQ processes. Public bidding normally asks interested suppliers to purchase the RFQ; this process has its benefits and losses, as detailed in Table 3.1.

Table 3.1: Advantages and disadvantages of having participation fees for RFQs.

Serial#	Advantages	Disadvantages
1.	Customer knows the potential bidders.	Knowing bidders in advance can create up-front preference toward a particular bidder.
2.	Participation fee involvement attracts only interested, experienced bidders.	Participation fees may demotivate new bidders, as they have less know-how of customer preferences and risk losing money for buying an unnecessary RFQ.
3.	High-participation fees attract only competitive suppliers.	Bidders will load the cost of buying tender in their quotation only, or any other running project offers.

CHAPTER 4

Bid Evaluation

Bid evaluation decides on the preferred supplier for meeting the customer's requirements. Deciding on a particular supplier is not an easy task, especially if we are working in a matrix environment where the procurement role is more of a support role. There are then several steps to complete the bid evaluations.

4.1 Types of Bid Evaluations

As discussed earlier, just as there are types of bidding methods (i.e., single-part and two-part bids), bid-evaluation steps depend on the bidding method. Who will evaluate the bidder's offer is based on the following bidding methods:

4.1.1 Evaluations of Single-Part Bids

The buying organization has asked for single-part bids from the bidder, which are techno-commercial offers that comprise technical, commercial, and price parts in a single envelope or email. This offers all the details in one go. Normally, such quotations ask for requirements with less technical complexity, although following a bidding method depends on the organization. Many private organizations ask for single-part bids to speed up the decision process, and this involves a high level of transparency in the procurement process, whereas for public organizations, fair evaluation is more important, since public money is involved; such offers are for simple project requirements with almost no technicalities. Figure 4.1 shows the flow for a single-part bidding process.

4.1.2 Evaluations of Two-Part Bids

Buying organizations first evaluate the technical and commercial bids with respect to the customer requirements or project requirements. Based on the technical bids evaluation of the bidders, only qualified bidders will be evaluated for price bids. So, for example, the buying organization needs to buy transformers for the project. First the transformer offers are evaluated for the technical and commercial part, and upon completion of technical and commercial evaluations, they are then evaluated on a technical comparative sheet. The commercial comparative sheet is generated and will be the output for opening up price bids. Suppose three bidders have submitted offers and only two have

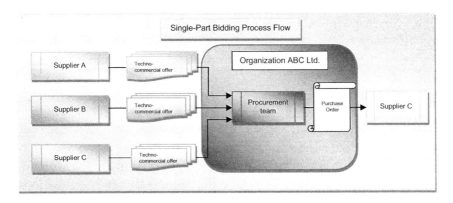

Figure 4.1: Single-part bidding process flow.

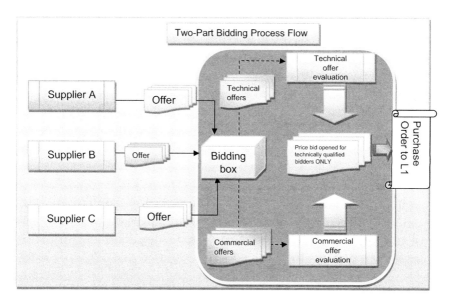

Figure 4.2: Two-part bidding process flow.

been qualified for meeting the technical and commercial requirements; then only these two qualified bidders will be considered
as qualified bidders, and their bids will be opened for price and
subsequent comparison. Disqualified bidders will not be considered for comparison on opening price bids. Figure 4.2 shows the
flow for the two-part bidding process.

4.2 Technical Comparative

As described previously (and shown in Figure 4.2), technical
evaluation is the criteria for decision making about the order
award. The technical comparative is the output of the technical
evaluation activity, which is supposed to be performed by a technical expert who is aware of the project requirements.

The expert performing the technical evaluation would require
a list of project requirements, the supplier offer, and the tools
to make a technical comparative sheet. The tool often used is
spreadsheets, like Microsoft Excel.

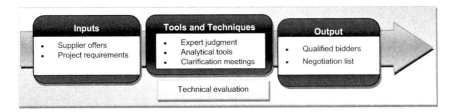

Figure 4.3: Technical comparative—input, tools, techniques, and output.

Although we can have more qualified bidders on commercial evaluations, the technical comparative will become an important tool to make a judicious decision. A sample technical comparative sheet is depicted in Figure 4.4.

4.3 Commercial Comparative

As described earlier, the process flow of commercial evaluation is the criteria for decision making rather than the order award. The commercial comparative is the output of commercial evaluation activity, which is supposed to be performed by a commercial expert who is aware of the project's commercial requirements.

The expert performing the commercial evaluations would require a list of project commercial requirements, supplier offers, and tools to make a commercial comparative sheet (refer to Figure 4.5). The tools often used to make such comparatives are a spreadsheet like Microsoft Excel, or less often, enterprise resource planning (ERP).

4.4 Decision Making

Outputs of the technical and commercial evaluation will become inputs for making the decision. Although it is good to have the best technically equipped supplier getting the order, that is not always the case, and the reason is simple. During the technical evaluation, the technical expert will make the best attempt to

Technical Comparative Sheet			
		Date	15 May 2017
Project	Supply, installation, testing, and commissioning of pressure vessel		
Project owner	EPC Ltd. New York		
Scope of work	Supply, installation, testing, and commissioning of pressure vessel		
Vendors	Supplier A	Supplier B	Supplier C
Qualification requirements	Existing Channel	Existing Channel	Existing Channel
Qualified on qualification requirements	Yes	Yes	Yes
General opinion	Genuinely interested in doing the job	Genuinely interested in doing the job	Initially, party has shown interest in executing the work, but during technical clarifications they could not demonstrate the execution skills for this job
Technical knowledge about intended job	OK	OK	OK
Knowledge of local standards and compliance	OK	OK	OK
A-class contractor license	Available	Available	Available
Statutory compliances	OK	OK	OK
Workshop facilities for prefabrication jobs	Not Applicable	Not Applicable	Not Applicable
Adherence to project requirements	Yes	Yes	Yes
Complete erection including all tests	Included in bidder scope	Included in bidder scope	Included in bidder scope
Competence for storage and unloading	Competent	Competent	Competent
Experience for executing the GIS work	Will be done through third party	Will be done through third party	Will be done through third party
Material disposal and adjustment of old equipment	Yes	Yes	Yes
Arrangement of earth-moving equipment like crane, hydra, fork lift, and so forth	Yes	Yes	Yes
Coordination with concerned authorities for vehicle movement during night hours	Yes	Yes	Yes
Preparation of storage area	Yes	Yes	Yes
Location of vendor	California	India	New York
Team competence	Yes	Yes	Yes
Recommendation	Technically acceptable	Technically acceptable	Technically acceptable
Final recommendations	Supplier A is nonlocal and coordination with vendor will be difficult and project execution might get delayed. Supplier B found technically capable but unable to demonstrate the job execution skills during technical discussion correctly, hence not recommended at this time for awarding the contract. Supplier C is local, and based on technical clarification meetings held with them, they are found qualified and are recommended for awarding the contract.		

Figure 4.4:   Sample technical comparison sheet.

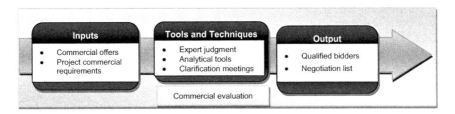

Figure 4.5:   Commercial comparative—input, tools and techniques, and output.

make the recommendation for the best supplier, but when it comes to deciding the order award, the procurement team has an altogether different target, which is to select the supplier with lowest-priced offers. Since technical and commercial comparatives will become inputs for opening the price bids of the technically qualified bidders only, there might be a chance that the lowest-priced offers have not been recommended technically for the project.

CHAPTER 5

Contracts

If you are an experienced buyer, then you must know the importance of the legal implications and terminologies for different types of contracts. The importance of contracts grows when such agreements or contracts are drawn up with international suppliers or contractors. It is the duty of the buyer to protect their own organization from unforeseen legal risks.

5.1 Difference Between an Agreement and a Contract

It is important for every buyer to understand the difference between an agreement and a contract. The very basic difference is that contracts are enforceable in the court of law, which means, in case of default by any of the parties, they are to be answerable in a legal trial, which further can lead to penalties, imprisonment, or both.

The world can be divided into two legal codes:

a) Civil law code: Decisions based on civil code are dependent on a compendium (which can be understood as a kind of encyclopedia), which has written defaults and decisions against each type of default.

b) Common law code: Common law code decisions are based on arguments, circumstances under which default has happened, and other unique situations. The decision of the judge is based on the trial hearing and/or earlier decisions given under similar cases.

From above, it is clear that lawyers are considered more important in common code law-based countries compared to civil code law-based countries.

Why it is important for buyers to know which country follows what type of legal code? The answer is simple: The buyer must know the risks before entering into or agreeing on a different law. For example, India is a common code law-based country, whereas countries in the Middle East are civil code based. In case buyers have limited knowledge of legal codes, it is always desirable to agree upon neutral country laws (i.e., third-country laws can be understood as laws that are neither from the buyer's country nor the seller's country). For example, if a contract is to be agreed upon between an Indian buyer and German seller, both may agree to Swiss laws (as they are considered neutral) as the applicable country for jurisdiction. Otherwise, it is desirable to have contracts agreed upon with countries having similar legal codes.

5.2 Elements of Contracts

Although there can be several opinions on elements of contracts, we shall discuss only the very pertinent ones. The important elements of contracts are:

- Offer and acceptance
- Obligations and consideration

5.3 Types of Contracts

It is of immense importance for any project buyer to know the available contract types that can be agreed upon with the subcontractor. For example, if company A is the project owner and has awarded the contract on a turnkey[1] basis (meaning from design phase to engineering, procurement, and construction projects, where the awarding organization will not participate in the completion of projects in a direct or indirect way), then contracted company B has to offload the contract in the best possible manner so that project profit margins can be enhanced due to subcontracted savings. The strategic buying team will have to decide the methodology for offloading the contracted works, either on a back-to-back basis (i.e., turnkey), a cost-reimbursable basis, and/or a mix of both, considering the potential risks by employing any particular type of contract. Therefore, the project buyer should know the following types of contracts:

- Fixed-price contracts
- Cost-reimbursable contracts
- Time and material contracts

5.3.1 Fixed-Price Contracts

This type of contract involves setting fixed prices for products, services, or results provided. Fixed-price contracts are beneficial for the buyer, as liability does not increase during the execution of work since the price is already fixed for the services, results, or product provided. However, such contracts can have incentive provisions for exceeding the contracted results. Sellers are at financial risk to complete the contracted work, and to meet the contracted requirements on time and within cost and scope. The fixed-price contracts can have the following subtypes:

- Firm fixed-price contracts
- Fixed-price incentive fee contracts
- Fixed-price with economic price adjustments

---

[1] *Turnkey* refers to complete works, which may include but are not limited to design, engineering, supply, installation, testing, and commissioning of materials at project sites.

5.3.2 Cost-Reimbursable Contracts

It is helpful to understand why sellers and buyers agree to cost-reimbursable contract types. The reason is simple; whenever scope or quantity of work is not clear, it is always advised to have cost-reimbursable contracts. Let us take a simple example. The project owner of company A has awarded work on a turnkey basis to an EPC (engineering, procurement, and construction), company B, to build a power plant. The EPC company has awarded the contract to different manufacturing companies for:

- Supply of turbines from the original equipment manufacturer (OEM),
- Civil works for installation of the turbine to another civil contractor, and
- Supervision services from the OEM required during installation of turbines.

In the above scenario, the number of supervision days cannot be estimated in advance, as the installation of turbines will depend on the contractor who is installing the turbine in the turbine-hall building. Therefore, while awarding supervision of works to the OEM, it is necessary to award such contracts on a man-day charges basis. It is important to understand why any EPC company requires supervision from the OEM. The reason is simple: In order keep the warranty terms intact, it is necessary to install the equipment in the presence of the OEM's supervisor to avoid any warranty issues. (However, there might be supply contracts which may insist on getting the equipment installed by the OEM only.)

This category of contracts is based on actual costs incurred plus the profit margin to the service provider. These types of contracts are beneficial for the buyer and seller, and are considered to be a fair arrangement, as the cost will always remain on an actual basis. Hence, such contracts are clear for both sides; however, such contracts are not favorable contracts for turnkey arrangements, as costs are always uncertain and may exceed due to any unavoidable delays. Now, think of a situation where the buyer has agreed to a turnkey arrangement with the customer, and offloads the contracts on a cost-reimbursable basis to the contractor. Then, chances are high for financial cost increases or fluctuations during the execution of works. These categories of contracts further have three subtypes, as follows:

- Cost plus fixed fee
- Cost plus incentive fee
- Cost plus award fee

5.3.3 Time and Material Contracts

Time and material contracts are a hybrid type of contractual arrangement that contain both the aspects of fixed-fee and cost-reimbursable contracts. They are often used for staff augmentation, acquisition of experts, and any outside support when a precise statement of work cannot be quickly prescribed. These types of contracts resemble cost-reimbursable contracts, as they can be left open-ended and may be left open for cost increases by the buyer. The buyer can leave the full value of the contract and quantity undefined at the time of the contract. Hence, time and material contracts can increase in contract value as if they are cost-reimbursable contracts. Many organizations require value and time limits placed in time and material contracts to prevent unlimited cost growth. Therefore, time and material contracts are fixed-unit price contracts when certain parameters are specified in contracts. To understand time and material contracts better, let us take an example of contracts that are based on price variations with time. For example, an organization would like to take EHV (extra high voltage) cables, where the price of copper will vary with time. So, the buying and selling organization will agree on the current prices in the market and drive the unit price applicable as on date. These organizations will utilize the price variation formula, which will decide the unit price at any future time for the copper cables.

5.4 Important Contract Terms and Conditions

Although every written word in the contract is of great importance for the execution of work, knowing the critical terms and conditions will make life easier for the project buyer, especially in a situation where the buyer is handling more than one project. Buyers discuss terms and conditions with their suppliers day in and day out, so they have to be aware.

Contractual terms and conditions are important for the customer as well as the contractor organization.

5.4.1 Termination Clause

Why is a termination clause important? Because disputes may arise in the absence of one. Contract termination can occur in two possible ways:

a) Termination by convenience: Termination of contract with convenience is agreeable to both the parties; reasons for termination may include project cancellation, end customer issues, because of a statutory issue, or any other issue where both the involved parties agree to come out of the contract.

b) Termination of contract because of nonperformance by one party: Termination of contract can be because of nonperformance of any member of the party against the agreed upon contractual terms. Such termination is always followed by a termination schedule, which will be time based.

The following is an example of what a standard termination clause may look like:

The customer (purchaser) shall be entitled to terminate this agreement by giving three-months' notice to the supplier in that behalf, without assigning any reason. All the obligations undertaken prior to such termination shall survive. After receipt of such a notice, the supplier shall not process the said products and forthwith hand over all the machines/tools/ drawings, etc., which are in the supplier's custody, along with the product processed by the supplier and remaining in the supplier's custody.

5.4.2 Payment Terms

We need to consider engineering milestones of the works, while agreeing to the payment terms. To understand this scenario, let's consider the following situation: End customer A has awarded the contract for building the complete electric substation to EPC contractor B, and B has offloaded the works for the supply of transformers to the manufacturing company, while installation goes to a third-party contractor. Therefore, party B has to take care of their payment from A before awarding the contract to party C.

5.4.3 Defects Liability Clause

A defects liability clause should be understood as a measure in the event that defects are found in the goods and/or services provided by the selling organization. The defects liability clause covers any risks related to supplied goods and/or services for a specified period of time.

Since products manufactured by organizations are specialized products for which these selling organizations have resources to upkeep such products, the buying organizations bind the selling organization for a period of time in which the selling organization will keep the product working for the agreed upon defects liability period without any cost, expense, and risks for the buying organization.

Standard defects liability clauses are discussed in the following sections.

5.4.4 Law of the Land

As discussed earlier in this chapter, the world can be divided into two legal codes. Ones that are based on civil law, and others that are based on common law. Countries that were ruled by the United Kingdom are common law. In common law, decisions of the court are based on decisions taken earlier in similar matters, where judges can refer to precedence to pass judgment on issues, whereas civil law-based countries refer to written decisions by categorizing the disputes and passing judgment based on a written law encyclopedia. Therefore, it becomes of immense importance that buying and selling organizations agree to the law of the land applicable in contracts for sale, which will become mandatory to refer to in case disputes arise. During the execution of contracts, the agreed upon law of the land will prevail.

The following is an example of what a standard law of the land clause may look like:

All sums payable by the customer (purchaser) to the supplier, or by the supplier to the purchaser under this order shall be due and payable at the customer's office. This purchase order shall be governed by and construed in accordance with the laws of India.

5.4.5 Dispute Resolution and Arbitration Clause

An arbitration clause is important because this is the resolution taken prior to approaching a court of law to settle a dispute between the seller and buyer. However, if an arbitration decision is not acceptable to either party (i.e., the seller or the buyer), then the parties have a right to move to a court of law. This process will avoid high litigation costs and valuable time.

The following is an example of what a standard arbitration clause may look like:

All disputes arising out of or in accordance with this contract, including any question regarding its existence, validity, or

termination, shall, unless amicably settled between the par-
ties, be finally settled by arbitration. The parties shall mutually
appoint a sole arbitrator who shall be a person who must have
held an office of a judge in any court of law. Notwithstanding to
what is stated above, if the parties cannot mutually agree upon
an arbitrator within 4 (four) weeks, then the customer shall
appoint a sole arbitrator who has held the office of a judge in
any court of law.

Each party submits to the jurisdiction of the court of law
for the purposes only of compelling compliance with the above
arbitration provisions and for enforcement of any arbitration
award made in accordance with the above provisions.

5.4.6 Time for Completion

This clause sets the time for delivery of obligations and/or services under the contract. This is a reference clause for having liquidated damages agreed upon (discussed in the next section).
Milestone dates, as well as completion dates, can become part of
time for completion.

Under civil law, the customer will not be entitled to liquidated
damages if the customer has prevented the contractor from completing the works within the agreed-upon date. Hence, at large,
time for completion is purely an approach for common law-based
contracts, as it will not fit into civil law, where time extension is
usually not a considered claim.

5.4.7 Liquidated Damages

Liquidated damages are compensation for the delays caused by
the seller in delivering the goods and/or services within the time
for completion. The delay damages are considered a genuine,
pre-estimated lump sum for failure to comply with time for completion. Delay damages should not be confused with penalties, as
penalties are fixed and do not have any basis for losses due to deliverable delays. In common law court, contracts with an agreed

upon penalty clause in the sales contract will not stand, as the penalty is already agreed upon between the selling and buying organizations. Therefore, such sales contracts require no discussion, whereas liquidated damages need to be established and proved in the court of law by the buyer. When liquidated damages are established and proved in the court of law, they need to be borne by the seller.

The following is what a standard liquidated damages clause may look like:

Delivery time is the essence of this contract and must be strictly adhered to. If the supplier fails to deliver the goods in time, the customer (purchaser) may, at its sole discretion:

a) *Treat the order as canceled at any time and recover any loss or damage from the supplier; or*

b) *Purchase the goods ordered or any part thereof from other sources on the supplier's account, in which case, the supplier shall be liable to pay the purchaser not only the difference between the price at which such goods have been actually purchased and the price calculated at the rate set out in this order, but also any other loss or damage the customer may suffer; or*

c) *Accept the late delivery, subject to deduction in payment of 1% of the total contract price for every week or part thereof of the delay, toward liquidated damages, subject to a maximum deduction of 10% of the contract price.*

For the purpose of establishing the timeliness for deliveries involving installation, commissioning, or recertification services, the relevant point in time shall be the date of acceptance.

5.4.8 Force Majeure

A force majeure clause voids all the agreement terms especially related to time for completion, as force majeure should be understood as abnormal conditions during which the seller or buyer fails to comply with the agreed-upon terms and conditions under the contract of sale.

The following is what a standard force majeure clause may look like:

The customer (purchaser) shall be under no liability for failure to accept the deliveries of goods, if such acts of failure are due to any act of God, fire, earthquake, floods, or any natural calamities or transportation embargoes, civil commotion, riots, violent acts of terrorists, state enemies, or any other similar reasons or circumstances beyond the control of the customer.

Such occurrence shall be informed in writing by the supplier.

5.4.9 Subcontracting

Major issues in the contractual agreement are related to product quality or workmanship of the works executed by the supplier. To avoid any use of contaminated services and/or goods, buying organizations have an exhaustive contractor qualification process where they audit the contractor's works for the existing product manufacturing and quality processes followed by the selling organization. On the other hand, it is impossible in projects that the single-selling organization can execute the complete works themselves; and hence, they offload partial or complete works. Such offloading will jeopardize the supplier qualification process and the customer may have issues during project executions. Hence, it is important to bind the seller contractually so that they may not be offloading the works. And in case they have to offload, they should receive prior approval from the customer, where the customer has the right to audit the subcontractor also.

The following is what a standard subcontractor clause may look like:

Subcontracting to third parties shall not take place without the prior written consent of the customer (purchaser) and therefore, entitles the customer to cancel the contract in whole or in part and claim damages.

5.4.10 Code of Conduct

The code of conduct clause is of immense importance, as it binds the selling organization to their behavior during the pre-award, execution, and warranty period under the sales contract. Such a clause will cover topics related to binding under the labor laws, bribery, and prohibition of child labor.

The following is an example of what a standard code of conduct clause may look like:

This code of conduct defines the basic requirements placed on the customer's suppliers of goods and services concerning their responsibilities to their stakeholders and the environment. The customer reserves the right to reasonably change the requirements of this code of conduct due to changes of the customer compliance program. In such an event, the customer expects the supplier to accept such reasonable changes.

The supplier declares herewith:

- *Legal compliance*
  - *To comply with the laws of the applicable legal system(s).*
- *Prohibition of corruption and bribery*
  - *To tolerate no form of, and not engage in, any type of corruption or bribery, including any payment or other form of benefit conferred*

upon any government official for the purpose of influencing decision making in violation of law.

- *Respect for the basic human rights of employees*
  - *To promote equal opportunities for, and treatment of, its employees irrespective of skin color, race, nationality, social background, disabilities, sexual orientation, political or religious conviction, sex, or age;*
  - *To respect the personal dignity, privacy, and rights of each individual;*
  - *To refuse to employ or make anyone work against their will;*
  - *To refuse to tolerate any unacceptable treatment of employees, such as mental cruelty, sexual harassment, or discrimination;*
  - *To prohibit behavior including gestures, language, and physical contact that is sexual, coercive, threatening, abusive, or exploitative;*
  - *To provide fair remuneration and to guarantee the applicable national statutory minimum wage;*
  - *To comply with the maximum number of working hours laid down in the applicable laws; and*
  - *To recognize, as far as legally possible, the right of free association of employees and to neither favor nor discriminate against members of employee organizations or trade unions.*
- *Prohibition of child labor*
  - *To employ no workers under the age of 15 or, in those countries subject to the developing country exception of the ILO Convention 138, to employ no workers under the age of 14.*

- *Health and safety of employees*
  - *To take responsibility for the health and safety of its employees;*
  - *To control hazards and take the best reasonably possible precautionary measures against accidents and occupational diseases;*
  - *To provide training and ensure that employees are educated in health and safety issues; and*
  - *To set up or use a reasonable occupational health and safety management system.*
- *Environmental protection*
  - *To act in accordance with the applicable statutory and international standards regarding environmental protection;*
  - *To minimize environmental pollution and make continuous improvements in environmental protection; and*
  - *To set up or use a reasonable environmental management system.*
- *Supply chain*
  - *To use reasonable efforts to promote among its supplier's compliance with this code of conduct; and*
  - *To comply with the principles of nondiscrimination with regard to supplier selection and treatment.*

5.4.11 Order Acknowledgment

Once the seller and buyer agree on the contract terms and conditions, including obligations and consideration for each party under the contract, then it is important to agree upon and acknowledge the sales contract in writing by both parties.

The following is an example of what a standard order acknowl-edgment clause may look like:

The customer may cancel the order if the supplier has not confirmed acceptance of the order (confirmation) in writing within (2) two weeks of receipt of the purchase order. If the terms of the confirmation vary from the terms of the order, the purchaser is bound by the general terms and conditions of the supplier only to the extent that these are in accordance with the purchaser's own general terms and conditions or if the customer (purchaser) agrees to such in writing. The acceptance of deliveries or services, as well as payment, does not constitute such agreement.

Any amendments or additions to the order shall only be effective if the customer (purchaser) confirms in writing.

CHAPTER 6

The Game of Negotiation

Like it or not, you are a negotiator like everybody else. This is a fact of life; everybody is negotiating all the time. You discuss a raise in your salary or position (or both) with your boss. You try to agree with a stranger on a price for his house. Two lawyers try to settle a lawsuit arising from a small fight or car accident. A group of power equipment manufacturing companies plan a joint venture for bidding for a steam power plant. A police commissioner of the city meets with union leaders to avert a transit strike. The Indian Minister for External Affairs sits down with his Pakistani counterpart to seek an agreement for limiting nuclear missile use against each other. All of these are negotiations.

Everyone negotiates for something with someone every day. We negotiate even when we are not thinking about it. A husband negotiates with his wife about where to go for dinner and with his child about when he should go to bed. Negotiation is the basic and only means of getting what you want from others; here, the point to remember is that one party is trying to negotiate what the party already has. It is back-and-forth communication designed to reach an agreement—when you and the other side have some interests that are shared and others that are opposed.

6.1 Fifteen Tactics and Countertactics to Win the Negotiation "Game"

We are negotiating all throughout our life. There is not a single moment when we are not doing it. Somebody is negotiating somewhere on some matter, and these matters may include personal, professional, and diplomatic issues. We even negotiate when we ask for a higher salary, benefits, or to transfer to another business unit or department. We negotiate employment terms and conditions, including salary, roles, and responsibilities with the future employer. We negotiate at home with children on matters of their interests; we often lose all such negotiation battles because children are very persuasive.

Countries often negotiate on matters of common interests, including creating trade-free zones, entering into double taxation avoidance agreements, and lesser duties on some commodities, or they negotiate to resolve disputes, including decisions on whether or not to isolate border areas from armies, to promote nuclear weapons for their first use by one country on the other, and so forth.

A successful professional negotiator understands the importance of cultural differences and prepares negotiations keeping these differences in mind. In India, while shopping in local markets, it is a tradition to ask for a double-digit discount; but in some other countries, it is not the tradition at all.

Negotiations cannot be avoided, as others will inevitably drag us into the negotiations.

This chapter will touch on traditional negotiation tactics and countertactics. We will explain the need for these tactics and countertactics. Negotiations are effective ways to arrive at conclusions, where all parties will agree to the outcome of the negotiations, but sheer information to participate as a negotiator may create feelings of insecurity about the results. The one who is strongest in negotiations will turn the results in their favor.

Negotiation has long endured an image problem. It evokes emotions related to conflict, dishonesty, and stress. A popular view of negotiation holds that it is merely the evolved version of barbarian welfare, where the more powerful, better armed, and psychologically superior negotiator engages only in winner-takes-all brutality. (Menard, 2004)

It is a back-and-forth communication designed to reach an agreement when you and the other side have some interests that are shared and others that are opposed (as well as some that may simply be different). More and more occasions require negotiation; conflict is a growth industry (Fisher, Ury, & Patton, 2011). Negotiation is a process of reaching an agreement, including terms and conditions, considerations, and scope of work, where such conclusions are acceptable to the negotiating parties.

6.1.1 Reject the First Offer

This is the first thing you can say even without having a detailed look at the offer. If you are salesperson, then you have heard this already: The customer says, "Your offer is many times their estimate and they will not be able to proceed further. Kindly correct the offer before we react to it." The customer does not have to put much effort in to get the first-level discount here and major corrections from the bidder. A countertactic is to dig for more strategic information on the submitted offer from the customer to know if they are bluffing or not. This tactic is mastered by the customer, as you might not be shortlisted further for evaluation if they are honest and not bluffing. The bidder should be ready to offer corrections after knowing the strategic points, where the customer is quoting the bidder's offer higher than their estimate.

6.1.2 Overlooking

When you are being pulled into a negotiation, you have two choices: you can overlook the request, or you can cancel the request. When your customer is trying to get hold of you to negotiate for an improvement in terms and conditions or for reduction in pricing, you may behave as if you didn't even hear their request.

This is especially easy for contractors to do, if you are trying to negotiate by email or fax. Ignorance is the popular tactic followed by contractors (or sometimes by the customer if the contractor is looking for a change order during project execution). Generally, this approach is followed by a trainee negotiator and is not useful except in delaying the real negotiation.

6.1.3 Deflect

When you negotiate for a reduction in price and an improvement in terms and conditions, a common tactic is to deflect your attention to another business issue for which you might not be responsible. It is very common that when a contractor is discussing something with the customer's technical person, they will try to divert attention to commercial issues, which may include payment issues or any other issue. On the contrary, when discussing with the customer's commercial team, the contractor may say, "I can't really discuss price until I understand how the technical arrangement will work and the value that you are seeking to get out of the arrangement." A countertactic is to negotiate collectively and not in isolation.

6.1.4 Deferral

When you negotiate for an improvement in pricing or terms, a contractor representative will often say, "I gave you the best price/terms that I am allowed to give. I'll have to check with senior management to see if we can do any better." This is where the contractor creates the impression that nothing further can be accomplished through the conversation; the contractor gets you to stop negotiating in the hopes that you will not ask again before awarding the order or contract. Hammer down such requests by saying that, "We are deciding the order shortly and you have to inform us of your final decision within the next few hours." This will shift the pressure to the contractor, and allow you to know the bottom-line offer.

6.1.5 No Negotiation

This is not a tactic, but a regulatory requirement laid by the government. Here the customer is the government organization, and as they are using public money, they cannot negotiate at their discretion. Government organizations are supposed to give all the bidders a fair chance, irrespective of the official's inclination toward any specific bidder. For high-value contracts, the bidding process is also a two-phase process, where the bidders are qualified technically and commercially, and, at last, the price bid of technically shortlisted bidders is opened. Whoever is lowest will get the order.

6.1.6 Splitting the Difference

This approach especially is used when both sides of the party are not ready to accept the other party's opinion or claim completely. This approach is often used when we are executing the project and a dispute arises for reasons such as an unclear and improperly written contract order, where the contract order deliverable is not identified clearly and in detail. Such a situation is normally handled by splitting the share between the contracting parties; it may be 50–50 or any other ratio. The first challenge is to bring all the affected parties to the table, as nobody is ready to accept the responsibility for the unidentified deliverable. This approach can also be used in other phases of the project. Normally, a "splitting the difference" tactic is used when negotiating parties found that it was nobody's fault or obligation. Therefore, in order to arrive at the conclusion, it is agreed upon to share the costs. However, the one who makes the offer to the other party will have to leave it to other party to agree or not, so the first party may have the less effective position.

You never want to be the first to offer to split the difference. It transfers veto power to the other side and may worsen your position (Menard, 2004).

6.1.7 Negotiation After Award

The least desirable negotiation leaves an unpleasant taste with the contracting parties. Such a negotiation is generally carried out when one party realizes that they are at a loss and they have agreed to a contract price that is lower. The reason could be due to current market fluctuations, currency variations, budget problems, or some other reason. Such negotiations are least preferable. These negotiations hurt the reputation of the initiator after the contract award for unjustified reasons and are rarely successful.

6.1.8 Electronic Auctions

Electronic auctions are the latest negotiation tactics, most popular with organizations lacking an experienced and professional negotiator or project procurement teams. Many companies have come up providing these auction services at a nominal fee. Perceived benefits include saving time, effort, and money. Electronic auctions exist in various formats (e.g., Dutch auction, English auction, reverse auction, etc.). Generally, these are conducted after everything has been agreed to, including technical scope and commercial requirements, but excluding the price. As a rule of auctions, e-agreements are signed before logging onto the system. Other advantages of electronic auctions are that prospective contracting parties don't have to be face to face to negotiate a contract.

Good organizations need to decide wisely before implementing such auctions, as they can definitely get the better price (contractors are under pressure to be the lowest to win the contract) compared to traditional negotiations, but they create increased chances of claims during execution from contractors. Also, this is being misused by some small organizations.

6.1.9 Persuasion

Persuasion is important for all dealings, as nothing can be achieved without persuasion. A professional negotiator especially needs to be persuasive, because contractors know that weak procurement negotiators only ask for improvements to pricing or terms once, and often end up awarding the order or contract to the contractor. The negotiator should be determined enough to ask again and again, and again if necessary. By showing how important it is to get what you want, you will increase your chances of getting it.

6.1.10 Counteroffer

This is common negotiation tactic where customers smartly throw counteroffers to the contractor as a take-it-or-leave-it option. Sometimes it is good to make the counteroffer, but other times it is better to hide the target price.

6.1.11 Good Buyer, Bad Buyer

The "good buyer, bad buyer" tactic is very common and should be understood from the perspective of the seller, who is discussing a potential order with the buyer. The main feature of this tactic is that it is always played by a pair of buyers; the "good buyer" is always the one facing the seller, whereas the "bad buyer" (normally a deciding authority) is behind the scenes (i.e., the one who will never give any comfort to the seller).

The good guy/bad guy tactic is arguably the most barefaced. Virtually everyone has used it or has been abused by it (Menard, 2004).

The two main objectives of this tactic are:

1) To win the contractor's trust by being a good buyer (i.e., a good buyer has a good attitude, is open to understanding the contractor's issues, and is ready to understand the terms and conditions, or even the cost/pricing submitted by the contractor); and

2) The bad buyer generates fear during discussions with the salesperson. The bad buyer normally creates negative feelings in the mind of a salesperson, and hence the salesperson will take the feedback provided by the bad buyer seriously, as the bad buyer provides no assurance to the seller of getting the purchase order from the buying organization. The bad buyer may not be true and/or honest in discussions with the seller, but the selling organization has no option left but to believe the feedback provided by the bad buyer.

Roles can be better understood if you put yourself in a situation where you play the role of good buyer by front-ending the supplier, inviting quotations, and determining first-level scope clarifications and negotiation while your boss plays the role of the bad buyer who will appear in the final negotiation meeting. (You need to inform the supplier that your boss is the final authority and you can create more insecurity in the mind of the supplier by revealing that your boss doesn't like the supplier before the final negotiation meeting.)

The only countertactic to handle such negotiations is that if the bad buyer is present in the meeting, the contractor should not be afraid of facing them, and rather be more attentive toward the good buyer. The contractor should keep cool and calm and try to discuss issues only with the good buyer. Also, when a bad buyer is behind the scenes, the contractor should bring them out.

6.1.12 Demeaning

This approach is followed by some professional negotiators, but is often the customer's person who is higher in authority or the decision maker in the process. In this approach, the customer is not ready to give any respect to the contractor or his organization and is trying to keep the entire ground during negotiations. Such negotiators may keep the contractors waiting in the reception area for hours, or sometimes they offer a chair lower in height. If you find yourself in such a scenario, refuse such demeaning conditions politely and ask for another chair; also, the best approach to handle such negotiators is to treat the negotiator the same way, but with humility. And if you have to wait for more than 20 or 30 minutes, then you must notify him that you are leaving as you have another meeting lined up with another client, or you should not give him a sense of importance once the negotiation starts.

6.1.13 Exigency

This is the approach of professional negotiators when there has been a deadlock and the contractor is not ready to offer any further discount in terms and conditions or pricing. In such scenarios, normally the direct contact will call up the contractor and ask for his final offer, stating that the management approval meeting has started and the customer will decide in another hour. Because this urgent situation puts the pressure entirely on the contractor's shoulders, most often, the contractor offers a better discount as they treat this as their final chance; otherwise, they might lose the prospective contract order. The best approach to handling such urgencies is that you need to sense the buyer is bluffing; if so, then ask for more time, like five to eight hours to respond.

6.1.14 Authority Limits

This is one of the tactics applied by the customer when the customer senses that the contractor is not moving an inch.

Normally, the customer's procurement person states that they are not authorized to negotiate contracts over a particular value or cannot approve the contracts beyond a particular value, and if the contractor keeps the same offer, then he has to start from scratch and has to discuss the complete package with the customer's higher management. Naturally, the contractor feels trapped for two reasons: (1) the contractor is tempted to have the order immediately, maybe even on the customer's terms; and (2) the contractor doesn't want to start all over again.

6.1.15 Surprise

The surprise approach is also sometimes used by professional negotiators. In such cases, the contractor is made comfortable by notifying them that they have won the contract, and when the customer senses that the contractor is comfortable, he surprises him with either additional terms and conditions or a price adjustment. This approach is commonly followed by human resources departments, where an incomplete offer only mentioning the role and price is made to the prospective employee, but the all of the company's policies are kept hidden until such a time when the employee comes for the appointment letter.

All of these tactics and countertactics are used by one party with the other party. Since these are traditional negotiation tactics that everybody knows, they might not be very useful.

6.2 Project Phases Where Negotiation Strategies Decide Desired Results

Project business organizations can have many phases and these can be any number based on the organization's internal decisions to deal with projects. But, for simplicity and better understanding, we will divide projects into three phases, namely: pre-award, execution, and warranty.

Figure 6.1:   Project phases for negotiation.

6.2.1 Pre-Award

In this project phase, illustrated in Figure 6.1, the customer is discussing possible project requirements, including scope of work, deadline to project completion, licensing requirements, environmental clearances, health and safety instructions, and all other deliverables. Once all is agreed upon, the time comes to shake hands and sign the contract order.

The output of this phase will become the input to the execution phase, the warranty phase, and based on the contract agreement, work will be performed by the contractor and verified by the customer.

6.2.2 Execution

This is the phase where the contract agreement will become input to the execution phase. Now it's the contractor's turn to perform against the agreed upon deliverable, and the customer will verify the scope. This is the phase where all work is being done and performance reporting is initiated against the contract deliverables. During the execution phase, if the contractor is not performing well as per the contract, the customer has to look for other available options to get the project work done.

6.2.3 Warranty Phase

During the warranty phase, the contractor has performed against the contract and has handed over the work to the customer. If the work is acceptable by the customer, then the contractor has nothing to perform against the contract except to comply with the warranty requirements of the contract agreement. Normally, warranties are back to back, which means end customer warranty requirements are passed on to the end contractor to avoid all the risk of the intermediate customer or contractors.

Now, we keep these three project phases in mind and make an attempt to understand who has the upper hand in negotiation and during which project phase.

6.3 How and When to Negotiate Power Shifts During the Project

We are not living in a perfect world, where the customer always has the upper hand in negotiations just because they are customers.

There will be times when the customer can influence the results of the negotiations, and other times when the contractor will influence the results.

Therefore, it is important to understand who will influence results of the negotiations, and in which phase of the project. If we are aware of this power-shift curve in advance, then we will be able to decide our moves and steps carefully before starting negotiations.

It is evident from the curve shown in Figure 6.2 that the customer has the upper hand in the negotiation during the pre-award, as all of the bidders are in competition with one another.

On the contrary, the contractor becomes more and more powerful during the execution phase, as his or her involvement at the site increases as the project progresses. If we have squeezed our contractors to the maximum possible extent during pre-award, then this is the contractor's turn to trap us by submitting claims even for a small change, such as small changes to scope of work, terms and conditions, or some other reasons. Also, once the contractors are mobilized at the site, they get to know how their performance will affect the project and what is important

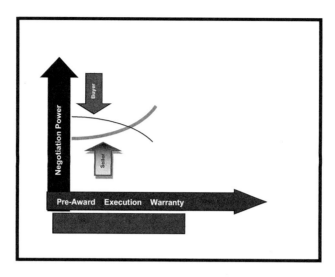

Figure 6.2:   Power-shift curve.

for the customer on the project. There, the contractor will make an attempt to tap all these opportunities, including additional work or big opportunities to recover for accepting small changes, which are sometimes totally unjustified, and the customer has no choice but to pay for these small changes.

You might ask why the customer would pay a mobilized contractor a large amount for accepting small changes.

One answer is in the question itself, which is that no one can meet the schedule better than the mobilized contractor, and the second answer is that the customer is lacking all the time to go back into the market and get this small change executed from a new contractor.

Termination of contracted work is definitely the least desired option, not only because of schedule constraints, but sometimes we have no other option, as the contractor has a monopoly in the market and is the sole source, or maybe the end customer's preference for the project. Also, beyond the threshold point as marked in the power-shift curve shown in Figure 6.2, the customer does not have much influence on the contractor. As the project acceptance date approaches, the project executing company has to meet the deadline agreed upon with the end customer, otherwise there will be huge losses and the project executing company has to pay high liquidated damages to the end customer. The liquidated damages or penalties may be many times the contract value of the nonperforming contractor. Moreover, this means less repeat business in the future from the end customer.

So, what will make the contractor perform beyond the threshold point? (The threshold point can be understood, in referring to Figure 6.2, as the point of intersection where the powers between buyer and seller meet during the execution stage and once the contract is awarded to the seller.)

Some may say we will go to arbitration and, thereafter, into litigation if required; these are the last options to confront disputes when negotiation fails. The process of arbitration is lengthy. If the decision awarded by the arbitrator is not acceptable to any party, then they can approach the court of law and further delay reaching a conclusion. There is no time to go through such a process when executing the project. So what should really motivate the contractor is consideration in terms of bonuses and incentives for mitigation measures. These are the only measures that can motivate the nonperforming contractor to start performing and finally achieve project milestones. Once the work is completed, the project is handed over to the end client. Therefore, the only priority during execution is to get the work done. Disputes between the contracting parties should be halted until then, and if required, the affected party should approach the arbitrator and subsequently the litigation.

The third major phase of any project involves a period for complying with the warranty requirements agreed upon under the main contract with the end customer. This is the phase where the contractor will decidedly have the upper hand, as no payment is withheld by the customer except as agreed upon under the contract. If you analyze this situation, the contractor has already created a buffer for these retentions while submitting the offer to you as their risk mitigation strategy. So, the retention or performance bank guarantee amount withheld by the customer is only a bonus for them, which they might like to have or they just don't care about it.

6.4 Negotiations Are Not Enough—Let's Understand Why

Negotiation tactics were very successful in the twentieth century, but not as much today. This is the era when we need to devise new tools and tactics to achieve better results.

Let's have a look at why negotiation tactics are not generating desired results.

6.4.1 Obsolete Tactics

Today, company executives are coming from top business schools where they have played roles in all of these traditional negotiation tactics and have mastered the art and science of them. Therefore, they know how to handle these negotiation tactics and come out as successful negotiators. We would not be wrong to say that these tactics have become obsolete in today's scenarios. Even if the executive is not experienced enough to handle these tactics the first time, they will recover losses from future projects. Therefore, it is advisable not to use these tactics when you want a long-term relationship.

6.4.2 Constrained Project Schedules

Project completion periods have shrunk compared to earlier days, hence the time lines for negotiations and placement of the order. Therefore, this is the time when you are not allowed to have a procurement order placement cycle time of 16 to 20 weeks. Today, procurement is supposed to place the contracts as soon as they have the approved purchase requisition, as the rest of the project milestones can be achieved once the resources have been mobilized to site.

6.4.3 Relationships Are Important

As time lines for completing projects have shortened considerably compared to the last decade, when time to completion may have been as much as five years. Now, we have only three to four years. Therefore, it is not desirable to do repetitive negotiations for different projects with the same party for similar requirements all over again. Vendor development efforts are part of the project procurement team and customer development is part of the sales team. Therefore, procurement personnel are tempted to misuse the contractor strategy to develop the customer, and the sales team is tempted to have the contract agreement from the new customer. In such a scenario, if the procurement personnel are strong enough in negotiations, they will influence the results and the contractor will have to make some sacrifices to have the contract order. Here, the procurement professional has achieved the targets in the short term even without much negotiation, but in the long term, the customer will have troubles due to more execution claims planned for them by the new contractor. Due to all this, the mutual relationship will be at stake once these claims are on the table for solutions. Therefore, a better approach is to create a long-term business relationship.

6.4.4 More Execution Claims

First timers fail to negotiate a better contract, as they are not familiarized with enterprise environmental factors. Enterprise environmental factors can be understood as including, but not limited to, the working style within the organization, the procedures to be followed for negotiation, negotiation authority with the buyer, approval hierarchy to be followed, and other issues that may impact the results of negotiations. If one party takes a loss on account of these factors, then there will be more claims going back and forth during the project execution stage, especially when this party has more influence to drive the results of negotiations in their favor.

6.4.5 Arbitration and Litigation

If the contracting parties are not satisfied with the contractual obligations and considerations created under the contract order because disputes have arisen during execution, then there will be more arbitration cases and, subsequently, increased litigation issues. Therefore, the attempt is to have more long-term relationships and fewer arbitration issues.

In view of what has been discussed, it is clear that we have no choice but to promote win-win situations for each involved party. The rules of the game have changed, and squeezing the contractor is no longer the preferred method, until or unless you don't have any choices left. Now, single-digit discounts are being considered a good discount, irrespective of the part of the world you are operating in.

6.5 So, What Are the Options?

Squeezing the contractor is no longer preferred because even if the contractor accepts the order under pressure irrespective of the customer's negotiation tactic, the contractor will very likely not perform well against the performance standards, as nothing comes for free. Gone are the days when negotiations used to generate better results and enhance direct revenue for organizations.

In fact, negotiation approaches are changing minute by minute. Now, negotiations are being conducted by having a long-term view, which not only includes the present project in hand, but also future projects. Therefore, contracting parties will make every effort to create better relationships, making project business profitable and ensuring sustainability.

6.5.1 Long-Term Agreements (LTAs)

The only possible solution to the issues discussed above is to create long-term relationships. Long-term agreements (LTAs) are the future of relationships between the customer and the contractor.

In long-term agreements, price, terms, and conditions are already agreed to, so the customer doesn't have to discuss the same standard set of terms and conditions again and again; hence, there is a reduction in order placement time, cost, and efforts. However, project-specific additional terms and conditions will be discussed, even if required for small changes.

6.5.2 LTAs Timing

In the project business, long-term agreements (LTAs) are made by the organization at the proposal stage, when the customer is bidding for a specific project, and even before that, in some cases, especially when the customer is only doing one kind of project, like engineering, procurement, and construction (EPC) companies doing only power projects. However, different industries can have different approaches or different nomenclatures in these agreements; the idea is only to secure more business through collaborations.

6.5.3 LTAs Structure

The long-term agreement structure solely depends on the organization's contractual arrangement with clients because of the associated risks.

If the organization is doing lump-sum turnkey (LSTK) projects, then they would definitely like to pass on the risks associated in executing the LSTK projects. Otherwise, for cost-reimbursable contracts, the EPC organizations may take a business call to have the LTAs on the LSTK approach or on a cost-reimbursable basis with their contractors.

This LTA structure solely depends on the kind of arrangement the organization would like to have with their contractor, whether they want to exploit the opportunities by taking more risks or to transfer the risks to contractors and just play it safe.

6.5.4 How LTAs Work

The approach is very simple. Where the long-term agreements are already agreed upon between the contracting parties, they will become the framework for entering future contracts. The future contracts can be for the same project or for different projects of the EPC company.

We would not be wrong to say that LTAs are at the heart of specific contracts and everything depends on them. The LTAs can be agreed upon for projects coming up in different parts of the globe or for different project locations within the same country. LTAs for projects conducted in different locations may be affected in terms of law, place of arbitration, transportation costs, and licensing requirements, among other factors that should be considered while framing long-term agreements.

Whereas the customer saves on time, effort, and money in agreeing on a long-term agreement, the contractor shares the same benefit. In addition, the contractor is subject to less competition in the market while quoting for individual projects, creating a win-win situation.

6.5.5 Benefits of LTAs

6.5.5.1 Savings on Time

The main benefit of these agreements is that they save time, which matters in enhancing the chances to win the project during the proposal/bidding phase. Also, time is saved in executing the projects if they have already agreed to terms and conditions beforehand. The contracting parties are experienced enough with one another's requirements, style of operating, and what matters for them. Therefore, if you are successful in saving time during bidding or execution, this will create additional free floats in the project, leading to projects completed comfortably on time and with an enhanced reputation in the eyes of the customer.

6.5.5.2 Savings on Effort

We have definitely put forth fewer efforts if we have agreed to everything beforehand. We can use this energy to create more time for value creation, which, again, enhances reputation.

6.5.5.3 Savings on Cost

As a project business contracting company, we have spent fewer man-hours during execution; therefore, we will be successful in saving on overhead costs, which would otherwise be required to maintain more manpower to discuss contracts during execution. This leads to competitive prices for the customer and more savings for contracting parties. This will also enhance the chances of winning more projects.

6.5.5.4 Relationship Remains Intact

The heat generated during negotiating the contracts is avoided, and the relationship is maintained. As negotiation is required for agreeing upon the long-term agreement, it is required only once. Here, the contracting parties are more than customer or contractor because they know they have to work for all other projects as well, and small issues can be ignored.

6.5.5.5 No Execution Claims

The main benefit of long-term agreements is that there will be no claims during the execution or any other phase of the project. Therefore, closing the project will be faster, easier, and without any renegotiations. There can be claims for the first time on the first project, but those will be eliminated completely for future projects, as the involved parties will be more aligned on expectations, requirements, and ways of working.

6.5.5.6 Repeat Business and Less Arbitration/Litigation

Such arrangements will definitely ensure repeat business as long as the long-term agreements are valid and not limited by any regulatory requirements for public projects.

Because the contracting parties have been experienced enough in executing the project under the long-term frame agreements, there are fewer issues of arbitration or litigation since both have already worked together to define the LTA.

6.5.6 Limitations of LTAs

Long-term agreements are better than the traditional approach of agreeing to contracts every time based on the specific project requirements. As everything has its pros and cons associated with it, similarly, long-term agreements too have cons. Some of the limitations include the following:

6.5.6.1 Good for Standard Project Requirements

Long-term agreements are useful only when you have a standard set of deliverables, which is hardly the case, as every project is unique in nature, including location, deliverables, and so forth.

6.5.6.2 Additional Terms and Conditions Agreements

Most often, the customer also has customers, and therefore, to avoid risks or to transfer the project risks to the contractor, a good approach is to have back-to-back arrangements, which means that obligations of the end customer are passed onto the contractor and then the intermediate customer is safe from any associated risks. It is very difficult to agree upon project-specific terms and conditions with the same price.

6.5.6.3 Regional Laws and Limitations

Projects of highly complex natures, which may involve building nuclear power plants in any country, have their associated law limitations that may require use of local contents (local contents refs to material and services arranged from the country where the project is being executed) to be utilized for the project. Such local laws may require 80% use of local material and services, or in some cases, 100%. There can also be limitations related to licensing and inspections of the material being imported into the country, so these long-term agreements may not be useful or viable in such countries if the contractor is not able to fulfill the regional or local law requirements.

6.5.6.4 Compliance with Laws

In almost all countries, there are laws that say to avoid any monopoly. You have to maintain a competitive bidding process, especially when dealing with government projects. In government projects, such agreements are rarely possible. Therefore, pre-existing or long-term contracts are not of much use. Time, effort, and money are spent in freezing the contracts in compliance with anti-competition laws or local regulatory requirements.

6.5.6.5 Risk of Being Beaten by Competition

When long-term agreements are long enough, supposing more than a year, the chances of becoming uncompetitive are higher. As the market for commodities and currency is dynamic, the cost of raw material is changing all the time. The consequences might be lost customers, especially due to price fluctuations, in the case of a downfall in prices of raw materials. Therefore, while agreeing to long-term agreements, it is desirable to agree on market fluctuations in the prices and not to agree on a lump-sum basis, which can make long-term agreements ineffective and useless. Special effort is required during negotiating long-term agreements to avoid such situations.

6.6 Let's Collaborate

This is the era in which more effort, time, and money is being spent to increase customer-contractor collaborations.

These days, customers and contractors sit on the same side of the table and are attacking differences collectively. They think of unresolved points as a common problem, where both parties are contributing to finding the solution.

Customer-contractors are no longer walking away from the negotiation table because of heated arguments. They now treat differences as a common problem.

The customer treats the contractor as a business associate starting from the proposal stage. Collaborating as early as possible can take the form of a memorandum of understanding (MoU), a customer relationship agreement (CRA), or anything else, but the target is to achieve a common goal.

Now customers are not wholly and completely dependent on the independent cost estimators for making a proposal to their customers, rather they are collaborating with their contractors as early as possible, where they are going ahead collectively and have a shared interest to win the project from the end customer. So, if the contractor's customer secured a contract from the end customer, then the contractor will also get their share for supporting the proposal phase and doesn't have to compete with others during the project execution phase.

The crux of such collaborations early on in the project is: "If I win, you will also win, so let's collaborate!"

CHAPTER 7

Contract Change Management

Changes are expected to happen during project execution, such as when the project management team takes over the project.

Contract change management is a best practice among the best organizations. Such organizations have formal methods for recording and approving changes by a team normally known as the change control board, which comprises the project sponsor, project management office, and other competent authorities.

7.1 Definition of Change

Any deviation from the project plan is suitable to qualify as a change to the contracted work.

Project team members can argue that any change required to meet the end customer requirements is therefore suitable to qualify as a "change," but this may not be the case with EPC organizations, as EPC organizations are based on scope, time, and cost, which have all been agreed upon with the customer before entering into project execution. However, the customer may be ready to pay for the changes by providing delivery extension and/or any additional payment to the EPC organization. Therefore, only changes that are agreed upon with customer will qualify as a "change."

7.2 Change Management Process Flow

Figure 7.1 illustrates the general change management process flow and clarifies how changes should be handled and approved.

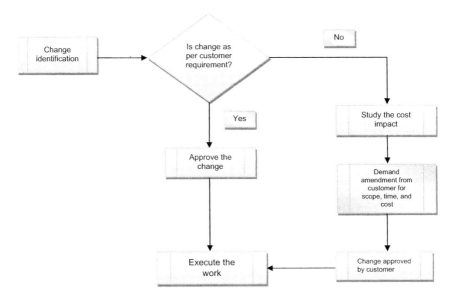

Figure 7.1:   Change management workflow.

7.3 Classification of Changes

Every organization can have its own classification for changes; however, based on experience and academic knowledge acquired in the last decade, we can classify them as illustrated in Figure 7.2.

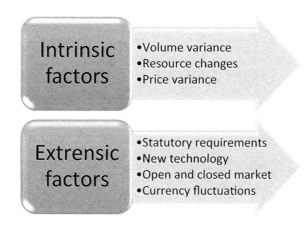

Figure 7.2:   Classification of factors responsible for contract changes.

Some of the project changes may occur because of intrinsic or extrinsic reasons like price variance; sometimes they are driven by fluctuations in the market for the price of the commodity, for example, if your project involves copper or any other commodity with a dynamic price. If the contract with the vendor does not have a price variation clause—and is not agreed to on a back-to-back basis—then the company will have to bear the hit. Therefore, price variance can be an intrinsic factor for change or it can be extrinsic to the project.

7.4 Managing Intrinsic Changes

Dealing with intrinsic factors depends on the maturity of the organization. Therefore, intrinsic factors can be managed, as they are dependent on the business decision.

The best way to do this is to pass everything on a back-to-back basis, although this is not always possible, since the value of subcontracts will change from 1% of the project value to 30% of the total project value (for organizations that have evolved from product to project). This underscores the importance of the risk management team.

The risk management team should consider all such risks and prepare the appropriate risk responses. For example, if an organization has to meet the project owner requirements for the project by subcontracting small supplies to a third party, then the risk management team needs to be sure enough that such a supply should not become critical for the project irrespective of the subcontracting value. In case this becomes unavoidable, then such requirements should have been identified at project inception and then risk response would be ready with the help of project procurement. Critical requirements, either small or large in value, should be identified earlier on in the project and a plan B should always be ready, in case plan A does not work.

The way to deal with price fluctuations is to have currency hedging; that is, if the commodity and/or services pricing depends on international currency variations. Although the finance team can have its own limitations regarding what is to be hedged or not, since hedging US$100 for a project valuing 50 million rupees is not a viable option, as hedging also involves cost. If the dependency is more than the threshold decided by finance, then hedge the currency to account for currency fluctuations. Another way is to hedge against commodities; for example, if you have a great amount of steel structure in a project, then you need to hedge your commodities, too. The quantity of commodities to be hedged has to be decided based on the organization's assessment of factors like project duration and past trends on prices of raw materials.

For LSTK contracts agreed upon with the project owner, there must be enough buffers for quantities that might not be assessable during the bidding stage and/or have considerable uncertainty for volume of variances during project execution. This is the only way for LSTK contracts to reduce the risk of losing margins.

There can be project situations that can have a great impact on project deliverables, and one of those reasons could be the resources, including people, materials, and machines, that are needed for executing the project. The project management team and risk management team should identify the critical resources needed for the project and must have a written risk response plan to deal with recourse changes during project execution. There is nothing in the world that is indispensable or for which there is no alternative. There is only the need to spend good time doing proper risk assessment.

Changed customer requirements can always be controlled, and this depends entirely on the effectiveness of the project management team. Every customer tries to "gold plate" the project without any costs paid for getting the gold plating done. However, if the project organization has not assessed the exact requirements for the project—even though they might have written detailed specifications or scope for the project—the only way to deal with it is to execute the project as agreed. However, there can be attempts to recover from inaccurate anticipations in another part of the project. Government project owners are always under the scrutiny of their regulatory bodies. Changes during execution are almost impossible, since public money is involved for such projects, and government officials who award the projects will be answerable for additional drainage of public money. Hence, while bidding for the government organization, the bidding organization needs to consider additional buffers for unanticipated requirements. They might be written into the contract or may be imposed through some government notification.

7.5 Managing Extrinsic Changes

These factors are external to the project organization and cannot be controlled, since they are not going to change, regardless of any decision taken.

For example, if the government imposes higher rates on import duties on material that is not available in the country, the project organization cannot do anything about it. Similarly, there are situations that change from open-market to closed-market conditions, for example, an organization cannot bring expats in on projects, since country law requires the organization to hire labor from the local labor union market.

Another example of uncontrolled factors is imposition of stringent environmental conditions to safeguard against pollution. This is something that cannot be controlled while executing the project; the only solution to such situations is to comply with the law, since the project organization has no option except to withdraw such projects if this is for its own purpose. However, if this is being done for some project owner other than the organization, withdrawing from the project will not be an easy task. Why? Because the organization's credibility would be at stake, and this can have a long-term impact on repeat business as well as on business from potential customers within that market.

So, what can organizations do to handle such conditions? All of us can agree that the only solution to handle such a situation is to have better project planning. In other words, while deciding the go/no-go for the project, the organization needs to consider long-term factors that can affect the project. This is the only way to eliminate such situations. Nothing much can be done, until or unless the government decides upon further changes, which may be in favor of the project organization—a rare possibility, since such changes happen only with a change in the federal government.

CHAPTER 8

How Finance Views Procurement Savings

Professional buyers have a clear view of their importance within the organization. They know that every single penny saved is not just a savings to the available budgets, but brings manifold benefits to the organization. In this chapter, we will have a look at the benefits of procurement savings from the finance perspective.

8.1 Benefits of Procurement Savings

Around the globe, there are many ongoing debates for capturing the exact procurement savings and their short-term and long-term impacts for the organization.

Even mature organizations compare savings with respect to the budgeted value. Procurement savings have the following impacts on an organization's financials (depicted in Figure 8.1):

- Working capital
- Bottom line
- Balance sheet

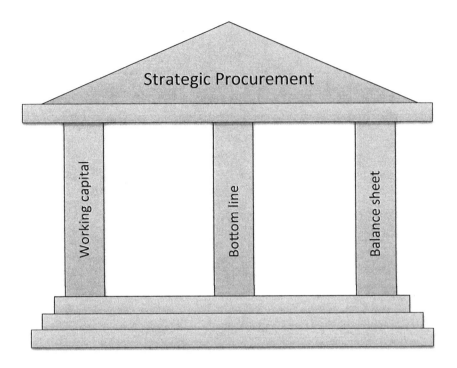

Figure 8.1:   Three pillars of strategic procurement.

8.1.1 Working Capital

Working capital is the amount of a company's current assets minus the amount of its current liabilities. For example, if a company's balance sheet dated June 30 reports total current assets of US$323,000 and total current liabilities of US$310,000, the company's working capital on June 30 is US$13,000. Therefore, it is obvious that a majority of expenses are incurred via the procurement cell of any organization, and in the case that procurement could save, say, an additional US$10,000, the organization's working capital will increase, which will lead to higher working capital. Furthermore, this means that the organization has to depend less on taking loans from banks and hence, saves on interest payments. In such a case, the organization's working capital will be US$23,000, which is shown in Figure 8.2.

Serial Number	Without Procurement Savings	With Procurement Savings
1	US$13,000	US$23,000

Figure 8.2:   Working capital with and without procurement savings.

From Figure 8.3, it is clear that the organization will have more spending power or operating money, which will be freely available and without any interest liability.

8.1.2 Bottom Line

A company's bottom line is its net income. The bottom line is a company's income after all expenses have been deducted from revenues. These expenses include interest charges paid on loans, general and administrative costs, and income taxes.

A company's bottom line can also be referred to as net earnings or net profits. The best thing about procurement savings is that they are a direct stream of revenue for the organization, which has been generated without investing any efforts or resources, and

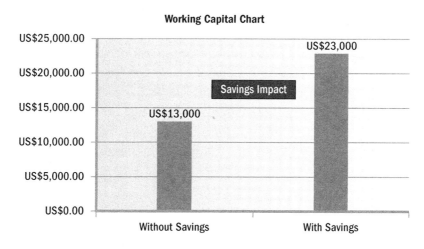

Figure 8.3:   Working capital chart showing increased capital.

above all, no taxes have to be paid on savings. Any organization has this as one of the main key performance indicators (KPIs) of their business, apart from sales revenue and collection of payments from the customer. So, the organization's performance will be measured on the following three parameters:

- Sales revenue
- Payment collection
- Bottom line

While bidding for any project, the tendering and business development team has to have the maximum hit rate, which is the number of orders received against the number of offers submitted by them (see Figure 8.4).

The sales team will keep pushing the tendering team for reducing costs in the offers because sales performance depends on the value of orders booked in a particular year. Think of the following: If the sales team keeps bringing inquiries, but the value of orders received is not as per sales targets, who is responsible for this failure? Is it the sales team or the tendering/cost estimation team? In this scenario, where markets for orders are decided on competitive prices, the costing team would be responsible. Therefore, a key performance indicator for the tendering team is the hit rate. The tendering manager has to be accountable for correct estimations; therefore, the organization should define a red line below which orders cannot be taken. For example, if the red line is defined as 15%, the organization will not bid on a project where profit margins are below 15%.

It is interesting to know where these costs are flowing to the tendering manager from. The tendering manager is responsible

HIT RATE = Number of orders received/Number of offers submitted

Figure 8.4:   Hit rate.

for considering all the costs going to the execution of projects, such as:

- Direct costs for material and manpower
- Costs for unforeseen risks
- Project management costs
- Costs for tax and statutory liabilities
- Profit margins after all costs

Every organization focuses on increasing sales revenue, as sales revenue is the first item on the income statement—and then all expenses are deducted from this figure. Therefore, organizations attempt to increase sales while trying to keep the expenses minimal, which is, again, a tough task to perform. The attention is on minimizing the expenses again, and this is possible by procurement in a more effective way, as procurement professional buyers are the ones who can control expenses. The procurement function is responsible for buying goods and/or services at the best rates, and hence, having direct savings from what is budgeted during the bidding stage will become the direct revenue stream and will contribute to a better bottom line.

Another way of looking at the bottom line is that it is the company's ability to pay back dividends to its shareholders over a specific period. However, dividend payout will depend on the dividend payout ratio. For example, if the dividend payout ratio is 60% and the organization has made a net income of US$100, then the organization distributes US$60 to its shareholders, and US$40 will be retained as the organization's retention income.

8.1.3 Balance Sheet

A balance sheet is an instrument or report on the financial health of a company. Every procurement professional knows the importance of the balance sheet, as they need to deeply study the potential vendors' financial health and, at the same time, they need to control and contribute to improving the balance sheet of their own organization. We will see how procurement savings helps the balance sheet; but first, let's look at what a balance sheet is.

A balance sheet is a statement of assets, liabilities, and capital at a particular point in time. In short, the balance sheet is prepared annually and can be correlated to a snapshot of a moving train. The balance sheet reflects the following equations (see Figures 8.5 and 8.6).

Total worth of company = Worth of shareholders/owners + Worth of outsiders' equity

Figure 8.5: Balance sheet equation.

It is known that any organization either includes the owner's funds, borrowed money, or both; we can rewrite the equation as:

Assets = Owner's equity + Liability of business

Figure 8.6: Assets and liability equation.

Assets maybe understood as the *amount invested* by the company to run different activities like procurement of machinery, land and building, fixtures, patents, and so on. Assets also include the money payable to the company by customers who have purchased goods and/or services on credit. The right-hand side of the equation shown in Figure 8.6 refers to the liabilities, which refers to the amount taken by the company from other owners/ shareholders who invest in the company with the intention to earn profits. Such amounts invested by the owners and/or shareholders are referred to as owner/shareholder equity.

Let us try to further understand what balance sheets look like for a new company that has just started in manufacturing

Liabilities		Assets	
Description	Amount	Description	Amount
Owner's equity	US$10,000	Machinery	US$15,000
Creditors	US$5,000		
Total	US$15,000	Total	US$15,000

Figure 8.7:   Balance sheet.

activities and needs to buy machinery for carrying out these activities. The cost of the machinery is US$15,000. The owner has
US$10,000 in available equity. The company needs additional
funds of US$5,000, which the company will borrow from the
bank. The balance sheet at this point is shown in Figure 8.7.

After the company has started operations and is making profits, all the money it makes after paying expenses, taxes, and interest to the bank will belong to the shareholders. Therefore,
whatever money the company makes will become part of the liabilities side of the balance sheet. On the liability side, the owner's equity will go up, whereas on the asset side, cash will go up,
keeping the liability and asset equation balanced.

Now, consider a scenario in which the procurement team of
this company negotiated the prices for the machinery, and procurement managed to buy the machinery at US$12,000. The re-
vised balance sheet will be as shown in Figure 8.8.

The revised balance sheet shows that interest on US$3,000
has been saved, and then the company has the option to either
reduce the owner's equity, pay the bank loan, or retain this cash
for future use. This shows that procurement savings improves the
balance sheet.

Liabilities		Assets	
Description	Amount	Description	Amount
Owner's equity	US$10,000	Machinery	US$12,000
Creditors	US$2,000		
Total	US$12,000	Total	US$12,000

Figure 8.8:   Revised balance sheet.

CHAPTER 9

Procurement Order Closure

Once a contract is awarded, that does not mean project team work is over. Almost every contract gets amended either during the execution of works or during the closure of works. It is an important task for the project procurement team to review these open orders on a periodic basis to arrive at the actual cost; otherwise, the profit margin cannot be calculated.

9.1 Importance of Procurement Order Closure

Normally, organizations book the purchase order received from the customer; this is called the sale order. Every sale order has the estimated costs entered against different heads, which were considered by the tendering team for a particular project, and are based on these estimated costs and received sale order prices; profit margins are calculated before getting the order from customer.

Table 9.1 depicts sample project margin calculations after consideration of various costs, which involve direct, indirect,

Table 9.1: Sample project margins calculations.

	Cost Elements	Plan (in Millions US$)
1	Project management	15
2	Labor production overhead	19
3	**Total direct labor and overhead**	**34**
4	Material external	4,842
5	Equipment external	
6	Purchasing internal	3,200
7	Subcontracting external	
8	Site materials and utilities	
9	Sourcing overheads	109
10	**Total sourcing and overhead**	**8,151**
11	**Total production (Row 3+ Row 10)**	**8,185**
12	Transport	
13	Travel and expense account	
14	Other insurances	
15	Bank charges	
16	Miscellaneous	
17	Other direct costs	
18	Warranty cost	
19	Risk analysis impact	**89**
20	Cost of sales	8,274
21	Selling price	(8,856)
22	Gross margin	**(582)**
23	Gross margin %	**6.58%**
24	Upstream value	(320)
25	Commercial gross margin value	(902)
26	Commercial gross margin %	**10.19%**

and other miscellaneous costs. Every project buyer has certain targets to determine savings, which are set as key performance indicators for any buyer; however, very few buyers know how savings secured by their effective negotiations will lead to project success. Projects are unique in nature, and calculations done by tendering will never prove to be correct, especially when moved to project execution teams. Therefore, in order to keep the project margin intact, the procurement team contributes by savings, whereas the execution team contributes by ensuring that purchase orders issued during the initiation of projects are closed on time, so that hanging costs will not impact the margins and they can have real-time savings from the systems.

9.2 Procurement Contribution During Project Closure

It has been a critical role of the procurement leader to review the open orders and keep reconciling them with fixed frequency. In a project job, a majority of the work awarded is based on the project situation at a particular time, which may change. Reviewing and assessing the open purchase orders is an important activity to keep the actual costs booked in a timely manner and to keep tight control on margins.

Start-up organizations that have only recently set up a project procurement team often miss the important activity of reviewing open purchase orders, and this is usually when they incur losses or start investigating the reasons for project margin losses.

CHAPTER 10

Financial Risks Analysis

Financial ratio analysis has been the greatest tool for evaluating the financial health of organizations. Because contracts involve several types of payment terms that can be agreed upon mutually during the procurement stage, the health of the supplier's organization needs to be evaluated even before considering them for the contract award.

The stock market and businesses in the United States, as well as a few other organizations across the globe, are superb because of the transparency offered to investors. Organizations publish financial data every year, along with their financial ratios, so that investors can decide whether to invest in the organization or not.

In the same way, financial ratios can be used to know how the supplier's organization is doing, what the efficiency of the people working within the organization is, how much they owe to investors, what their long-term or short-term liabilities are, and how they could meet these liabilities. The financial statement may have been the greatest tool ever.

10.1 Classification of Ratio Analysis

Ratio analysis can be classified in many ways, but for simplification purposes, it can be conducted in two ways, namely through trend analysis and comparative analysis.

Trend analysis is a way of knowing organizational health for the last five years, for example, which will let anybody know how the organization has been doing. Comparative analysis compares the last two years of the organization's financial health or any other organization with the same portfolio (see Figure 10.1).

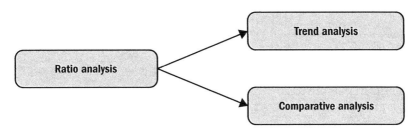

Figure 10.1:   Classification of ratio analysis.

10.2 Financial Ratios of Interest

Financial ratios can be calculated in many ways; however, for simplicity, we have tried to classify these ratios in the following ways. Figure 10.2 shows ratios that are more or less evaluated by a majority of financial analysts.

10.2.1 Solvency Ratios

Any organization can sustain for a longer period of time if they have enough cash, assets, and low debt. Any organization needs cash to employ resources, which includes manpower, machines, and materials—and all these resources can be employed if the organization has no financial trouble.

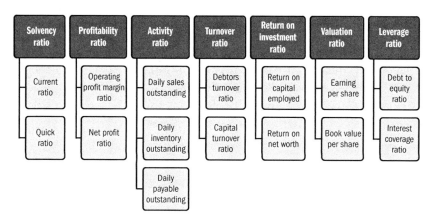

Figure 10.2:   Financial ratio types.

10.2.1.1 Quick Ratio

The quick ratio measures a company's ability to meet its short-term obligations with its most liquid assets. The higher the quick ratio, the better the position of the company (see Figure 10.3).

> **Quick ratio = (Current assets – inventories)/Current liabilities**

Figure 10.3:   Solvency ratio.

10.2.1.2 Current Ratio

This is an even simpler variant to quick ratio, and is used to determine the company's ability to pay back its short-term liabilities. If the ratio is below 1, it raises a warning sign as to whether the company is able to pay its short-term obligations when due (see Figure 10.4).

> **Current ratio = Current assets/Current liabilities**

Figure 10.4:   Current ratio.

10.2.2 Profitability Margin Ratios

The profit margin ratio, also called the return on sales ratio or gross profit ratio, is a profitability ratio that measures the amount of net income earned with each dollar of sales generated by comparing the net income and net sales of a company. In other words, the profit margin ratio shows what percentage of sales are left over after all expenses are paid by the business.

Creditors and investors use this ratio to measure how effectively a company can convert sales into net income. Investors want to make sure profits are high enough to distribute dividends, while creditors want to make sure the company has enough profits to pay back its loans. In other words, outside users want to know that the company is running efficiently. An extremely low profit margin would indicate the expenses are too high and the management needs to budget and cut expenses.

10.2.2.1 Operating Profit Margin Ratios

The operating profit margin ratio, also known as the operating profit margin, is a profitability ratio that measures what percentage of total revenue is made up by operating income. In other words, the operating margin ratio demonstrates how much revenue is left over after all the variable or operating costs have been paid. Conversely, this ratio shows what proportion of revenues is available to cover nonoperating costs like interest expenses.

This ratio is important to both creditors and investors because it helps show how strong and profitable a company's operations are. For instance, a company that receives 30% of its revenue from its operations means that it is running its operations smoothly, and this income supports the company. It also means that this company depends on the income from operations. If operations start to decline, the company will have to find a new way to generate income. The formula is given in Figure 10.5.

EBIT is the operating income, also called income from operations, and is usually stated separately on the income statement before income from non-operating activities like interest and dividend income. Many times, operating income is classified

$$\boxed{\text{Operating margin ratio = (EBIT/Net sales)}}$$

Figure 10.5:   Operating profit margin ratio.

as earnings before interest and taxes. Operating income can be calculated by subtracting operating expenses, depreciation, and amortization from gross income or revenue.

10.2.2.2 Net Profit Margin Ratio

Net profit margin is the percentage of revenue left after all expenses have been deducted from sales. The measurement reveals the amount of profit that a business can extract from its total sales.

The net sales part of the equation is gross sales minus all sales deductions, such as sales allowances. The formula is given in Figure 10.6.

$$\boxed{\text{Net profit margin ratio = Profit after tax/revenue}}$$

Figure 10.6:   Net profit margin ratio.

10.2.3 Activity Ratios

Activity financial ratios measure how well a company is able to convert its assets in the balance sheet into cash or sales. These ratios help us in analyzing how efficient and well run a company is. They measure not just the company efficiency, but also the people within the business and how efficient they are.

10.2.3.1 Days Sales Outstanding (DSO)

Cash is important for every business, and this ratio helps us analyze how fast business is converting the receivables into cash. The lower the DSO, the better the health and efficiency of the business. The formula is given in Figure 10.7.

> **Days sales outstanding = (Receivables/Revenue)*365**

Figure 10.7: Days sales outstanding.

10.2.3.2 Days Inventory Outstanding (DIO)

This ratio is used to measure the average number of days a company holds inventory before selling it. This ratio is industry specific and should be used to compare competitors. E-commerce companies like Amazon or Flipkart will have less DIO as compared to frequently moving consumer goods companies (FMGCs), as FMCGs need to have good inventory. The formula is given in Figure 10.8.

> **Days inventory outstanding = (Inventory/COGS)*365**

Figure 10.8: Days inventory outstanding.

10.2.3.3 Days Payable Outstanding (DPO)

Days payable outstanding shows the time, in days, that the business has to pay back its creditors. On the flip side, it also shows how long the company can utilize the cash before paying it back. The formula is given in Figure 10.9.

> **Days payable outstanding = (Accounts payable/COGS)*365**

Figure 10.9: Days payable outstanding.

10.2.3.4 Cash Conversion Cycle

Putting DIO, DSO, and DPO together, you get the cash-conversion cycle. The entire cash-conversion cycle is a measure of management effectiveness. The lower, the better; this is also a great way to compare competitors. The formula is given in Figure 10.10.

$$\text{Cash-conversion cycle} = \text{DIO} + \text{DSO} - \text{DPO}$$

Figure 10.10: Cash conversion cycle.

10.2.4 Turnover Ratios

Turnover ratios are financial ratios that measure an asset's activity or efficiency in generating or turning over cash. For example, inventory turnover ratio (cost of sales divided by inventory value) shows how many times an inventory was turned into cash during an accounting period.

10.3 Importance of Financial Ratios

The reason financial ratios are helpful for the buyer is simple: A smart buyer will peek into a vendor's business condition and can verify the state of affairs with the help of financial ratios.

It is common for the buyer to have multiple rounds of discussions with multiple bidders during discussions over one package award to the successful bidder. During all these discussions, clarification meetings, and qualification requirements, the purchasing organization has impressions of the bidders, which are helpful for arriving at the following conclusions:

1. Bidder's interest in the order and scope of work;
2. How competent the bidder is in managing the projects based on past performance for projects of similar nature;
3. How the bidder reacts to big and small changes during the project; and
4. Bidder's ability to be concise, clear, and keep good records.

However, not all of these impressions formed by the project buyer during the discussions may be correct, based on the following reasons:

- Salesperson is new to the organization and doesn't have knowledge of the organization's workings or past records;
- Past performance is very old and may be fabricated or is not an exact match with requirements;
- Sales leader is not very aggressive and less presentable during meetings with the project buyer; and
- Records are untidy because of non-preparation by new sales team members.

These financial evaluations validate whether the impression made by any buying organization is correct or not. We will evaluate the following ratios and try to analyze the impacts/risk for the buying organization.

- Current ratio
- Quick ratio
- DSO
- DPO
- Sales growth (not a ratio, but increase/decrease from last year's results)

It is better to revisit the ratios before making any analysis of the balance sheet.

You can think of the following when you get the results from an investor's point of view:

- **Current ratio** is the organization's capability to pay-back by selling all of its current assets. This ratio will give us preliminary results; this is nothing but the ratio of current assets to current liabilities.

- **Quick ratio** is a more refined ratio, and will consider only the immediate convertible assets into cash.

- **DSO** is the organization's capability to collect payment from customers; this is the best indicator of the organization's performance against the works. If the DSO is more than the industry standard, the DSO will let the buyer know two things:

  1) The bidding organization has documentation issues; or

  2) The bidding organization has performance issues, including the supply of materials or execution of work, because of which payment has been delayed by the customer.

- **DPO** (daily payable outstanding) is the ratio that tells us the bidder's capacity to payback their subvendor for supply of material and/or services received by the bidding organization. If this is higher than market standard, there are the following three risks:

  1) The subvendor-supplied material has quality issues, because of which material/services payment has been delayed;

  2) The bidder is unable to make payment to their sub-vendors; or

  3) The bidder's vendor may delay the raw materials because of payment issues.

- **Sales growth:** Every organization works to acquire more and more jobs from the market, so their top line grows exponentially. Sales growth tells the procurement organization the following:

  ○ The competitiveness of the seller;

  ○ The seller's performance in increasing business;

- ○ Current loading (orders in hand/backlog of orders) of organizations; and
- ○ Any changes in focus from increasing the current portfolio.

10.4 Balance Sheet Evaluation

Now that we have attained an understanding of different types of financial ratios and the possible conclusions that can be drawn from a few of the important ratios, we need to evaluate these ratios using data-run calculations and then analyze the findings. A sample balance sheet will help us arrive at an indication of the financial health of the organization.

Consider organization ABC, which is operating in the services sector and executing projects for clients. Sometimes, this organization takes contracts for the complete supply, installation, testing, and handing over of work to the client; and sometimes, they execute only erection work.

Table 10.1 shows a sample balance sheet for financial year 2017.

When we calculate the different ratios based on one financial year, this gives us the following picture, as shown in Table 10.2.

Table 10.1:   Sample balance sheet.

Fiscal Year (2017)	December 2017 (All figures in US$)
Liabilities	
Share capital	3,399,000
Share application money	
Reserve and surplus	124,069,285
Secured loans	—
Other long-term liability + provision	—
Unsecured loans	—
(From holding company in nature of share capital)	
Deferred tax	273,793
Total	**127,742,078**
Assets	
Net fixed assets	26,728,475
Long-term loans and advance for fixed assets	4,579,478
Noncurrent investments	258,432
Noncurrent assets	—
Deferred tax	—
Current Assets	
Inventories	7,421,228
Other current assets	280,639
Current investments	
Sundry debtors/trade receivable	69,125,438
Cash and bank balance	40,671,409
Loans and advances	16,753,322
Total Current Assets	**134,252,036**
Current liabilities	28,602,208
Sundry creditors	9,474,136

(continued)

Table 10.1: Sample balance sheet. *(continued)*

Less Current Liabilities	38,076,344
Net current assets	96,175,692
Misc. expenditure	
Total	127,742,077
Profit and Loss Statement	
Sales	66,986,594
Other income	3,937,827
Increase in inventory	–
Total A	70,924,421
Purchases	14,583,825
Other expenses	43,914,573
Interest and finance charges	2,622,500
Depreciation	1,619,769
Total B	62,740,667
PBT* Total A – Total B	8,183,754
Provision for taxes	2,548,290
PAT* 1	5,635,464

*PBT; Profit before taxes
*PAT: Profit after taxes

Table 10.2: Ratio analysis.

Serial#	Ratio	Formula	Result
1	Current ratio	Current assets/current liabilities	3.53
2	Quick ratio	(Current assets-inventories)/current liabilities	3.33
3	Net profit margin	Profit after tax/sales for the year %	8.41%
4	DSO	Sundry debtors/sales per day	377
5	DPO	Sundry creditors/credit purchases per day	237

CHAPTER 11

Incoterms®

What does Incoterms® stand for?

The word Incoterms® is an abbreviation for International Commercial Terms; these provide a common set of rules used for defining the responsibilities of sellers and buyers in the delivery of goods under sales contracts.

These rules were first published in 1936 and are being updated by the International Chamber of Commerce (ICC) in Paris regularly. Incoterms® are good for about 10 years. The frequency is not fixed, but this has been true historically. They are revised based on dynamism in the international trade practice. If the changes in international trade become very frequent, Incoterms® are revised to match international trade practices.

Incoterms® rules:

This is a set of three-letter trade terms reflecting business practices in contracts for the sale of goods.

Incoterms® rules define the responsibilities of sellers and buyers for the delivery of goods under sales contracts for both domestic and international trade. The following aspects are important to consider:

- The terms aren't law—there are no laws that require their use and they are not all-inclusive;
- They are country neutral—they don't favor one country over another; and
- They are self-contained—all information that determines responsibility and risk are in one place.

Incoterms® reflect worldwide trade practices, as practices change, Incoterms® are revised.

Incoterms® 2010 were written by the ICC, represented by eight individuals from various parts of the world, who:

- Met 11 times in person;
- Received over 2,000 suggestions in the first request; and
- Refined suggestions from four proposals.

The controlling source document is written in British English and will be translated into 35+ languages over the next year.

Incoterms® 2010 have been in effect since 1 January 2011.

11.1 Eleven Golden Rules of Incoterms® 2010 Publication

Below is a list of 11 three-lettered Incoterms®, published under Incoterms® 2010 by ICC. These abbreviations are to be incorporated into the contracts/agreements between sellers and buyers:

- **EXW:** EX-WORKS
- **FCA:** FREE CARRIER
- **CPT:** CARRIAGE PAID TO

- **CIP:** CARRIAGE AND INSURANCE PAID TO
- **DAT:** DELIVERED AT TERMINAL
- **DAP:** DELIVERED AT PLACE
- **DDP:** DELIVERED DUTY PAID
- **FAS:** FREE ALONGSIDE SHIP
- **FOB:** FREE ON BOARD
- **CFR:** COST AND FREIGHT
- **CIF:** COST INSURANCE AND FREIGHT

11.2 Key Benefits of Using Incoterms® Rules

These rules are an international standard and are accepted throughout the world. They have become part of global trade practice. Incoterms® provide clarity to sellers and buyers, which reduces the need to include detailed information in the purchase orders. Also, these terms provide a common platform for both the seller and buyer.

Transit damages have been the greatest concern while working with international suppliers. In case contracts are made up without any Incoterms®, it will be difficult to have a clear understanding about the transfer and title of goods, who will do the loading and unloading of material, and many other important points.

11.3 Buyer and Seller Worries

In the absence of Incoterms®, some key points to discuss before concluding a contract would include:

- Who *furnishes* the goods?
- Who *packages* the goods in a manner suitable for shipment (export)?
- Who *moves* the goods from the seller's factory to a port, airport, or border crossing in the seller's country?
- Who *arranges* for export clearance in the seller's country (if applicable)?

- Who *arranges* for main carriage (international transportation) from the departure port to the arrival port?
- Who *pays* for the main carriage?
- Who *insures* the shipment?
- Who *arranges* for import clearance?
- Who *pays* import duties?
- Who *pays* for on-carriage from the arrival port to the delivery destination?
- Who *arranges and pays* for country-specific documentation (e.g., consular invoices, inspection reports, licenses, etc.)?

11.4 Classification of Incoterms® Based on Mode of Shipment

11.4.1 Any Mode or Modes of Transport

This class includes the seven Incoterms® 2010 rules that can be used irrespective of the mode of transport selected and irrespective of whether one, or more than one, mode of transport is employed.

The following belong to this class:

EXW, FCA, CPT, CIP, DAT, DAP, and DDP

They can be used even when there is no maritime transport at all. It is important to remember, however, that these rules can be used in cases where a ship is used for part of the carriage.

11.4.1.1 Ex-Works + (Named Place)

Named place is generally the seller's location (or where the product initially ships from).

- Delivery – The seller delivers goods when placed at the buyer's disposal at the named place of delivery:
  - Goods are packaged, and
  - Goods are not loaded on the collecting vehicle.

- Seller risks – The minimum obligation for the seller; once packaged, there is a loss of control over transportation movement, where the package is finally received, and how the export or import documentation is presented to relevant governments.
- Buyer risks – The buyer bears all costs and risks involved in taking the goods from the named place.
  - Carriage: Buyer responsibility to arrange for pre-carriage, main carriage, and on-carriage insurance.
  - Neither party is required to insure goods.
- Export/import clearance – The buyer must handle all requirements and pay all associated duties and fees.

Note: This should *not* be used when the buyer cannot carry out export requirements directly or indirectly.

11.4.1.2 Free Carrier (FCA) + (Named Place)

Named place is generally:

- Seller's place of business
- Seller is responsible for having goods available when promised, packaged to the extent known or agreed, and loaded onto collecting vehicle
- Buyer is responsible for pre-carriage, main carriage, and on-carriage
- Another location on the seller's side (e.g., international airport, freight forwarder warehouse for consolidation, or another location agreed upon by the seller and buyer)
- Seller is responsible for having goods available when promised, packaged to the extent known or agreed upon, loaded onto the collecting vehicle, and pre-carriage until agreed upon location of material transfers from seller to buyer; subsequent pre-carriage, main carriage, and on-carriage

- Buyer is responsible for unloading pre-carriage delivering vehicle, main carriage, and on-carriage
- Contract of carriage – buyer is responsible for making a contract of carriage; however, if requested, or if the buyer does not give instructions in due time, the seller may contract for carriage on usual terms at the buyer's risk and expense
- Risk passes to buyer at point of delivery
- Insurance – neither party is required to insure goods
- Export clearance – handled by seller
- Associated licenses can be obtained and maintained under United States law
- Automated export system filings can be completed by the seller
- Import clearance – handled by the buyer—responsible for the customs formalities and any duties, fees, and other charges due upon importation
- FCA Incoterm® is most commonly used in international contracts

11.4.1.3 Carriage Paid to (CPT) + Named Place (on Buyer's Side)

- Delivery – seller delivers goods to a carrier or another person nominated by the seller, at an agreed-upon place, for transportation to the named destination on the buyer's side, appropriately packaged
- Carriage – seller chooses and pays cost of carriage to bring the goods to the named destination (the final location, not the destination port)
- Risks – seller bears all risks and costs incurred until the goods are delivered to the first carrier on the seller's side
- Export clearance – handled by seller
- Import clearance – buyer is responsible for paperwork and all costs
- Insurance – neither party required

Note: Risk of loss passes from seller's side to buyer, *but* cost is seller's responsibility to named location on buyer's side.

11.2.1.4 *Carriage and Insurance Paid to (CIP) + Named Place (on Buyer's Side)*

- Delivery – seller delivers goods to a carrier or another person nominated by the seller, at an agreed-upon place, for transportation to the named destination on the buyer's side, appropriately packaged
- Carriage – seller pays cost of carriage to bring the goods to the named destination (the final location, not the destination port)
- Risks – seller bears all risks and costs incurred until the goods are delivered to the first carrier on the seller's side
- Export clearance – handled by seller
- Import clearance – buyer is responsible for paperwork and all costs
- Insurance – seller is required to obtain minimum coverage

Note: Risk of loss passes from seller's side to buyer, *but* cost is seller's responsibility to named location on buyer's side.

11.2.1.5 *Delivered at Terminal (DAT) + Named Place (Buyer's Side)*

- Delivery – seller delivers goods to named destination terminal on buyer's side, packaged appropriately and unloaded
- Seller responsible for pre-carriage and main carriage
- Buyer responsible for on-carriage
- Risks – transfer from seller to buyer once goods are unloaded on buyer's side at terminal
- Export clearance – seller responsibility

- Import clearance – buyer responsibility—documentation and fees associated
- Insurance – neither party is required to insure

11.2.1.6 Delivered at Place (DAP) + Named Place (Buyer's Side)

- Previously contained elements of DDU, DAF, and DES terms
- Delivery – seller delivers the goods to the buyer at the named place on the buyer's side, appropriately packaged, but not unloaded
- Carriage – seller handles all carriage to named place on buyer's side
- Risks transfer from seller to buyer once goods are delivered to the named place on buyer's side
- Export clearance – seller handles
- Import clearance – buyer handles and pays associated costs
- Insurance – neither party is required to insure

11.2.1.7 Delivered Duty Paid (DDP) + Named Place (Buyer's Side)

- Delivery – seller delivers goods to the buyer, cleared for import upon the arrival of transportation, but not unloaded at the final destination
- Carriage – seller handles all carriage to named place on buyer's side
- Risks – transfer from seller to buyer once goods are delivered to the named place on the buyer's side
- Export clearance – seller handles
- Import clearance – seller handles and pays for any charges associated
- Insurance – neither party is required to provide insurance

11.4.2 Sea and Inland Waterway Transport

In the second class of Incoterms® 2010 rules, the point of delivery and the place to which the goods are carried to the buyer are both ports, hence the label "sea and inland waterway" rules.

The following belong to this class:

FAS, FOB, CFR, and CIF.

Under the last three Incoterms® rules, all mention of the ship's rail as the point of delivery has been omitted in preference for the goods being delivered when they are "on board" the vessel.

This more closely reflects modern commercial reality and avoids the rather dated image of the risk swinging to and fro across an imaginary perpendicular line.

11.4.2.1 Free Alongside Ship (FAS) + Named Place (Alongside Vessel at Port on Seller's Side)

- Delivery – seller delivers goods to buyer alongside the vessel chosen by the buyer at the named port of shipment, packaged appropriately
- Seller handles pre-carriage
- Buyer handles main carriage and on-carriage
- Risks pass from seller to buyer once goods are placed alongside the vessel on the seller's side
- Insurance – neither party is required to insure goods
- Export clearance – seller handles
- Import clearance – buyer is responsible for requirements and associated fees

11.4.2.2 Free On-Board (FOB) + Named Place (Loaded on Vessel at a Port on the Seller's Side)

- Delivery – seller delivers goods to buyer on board the vessel chosen by the buyer at the named port of shipment, packaged for shipment
- Seller handles pre-carriage

- Buyer handles main carriage and on-carriage
- Risks – pass from seller to buyer once goods are placed on board the vessel on the seller's side
- Insurance – neither party is required to insure goods
- Export clearance – handled by seller
- Import clearance – handled by buyer

Note: "Ship's rail" is no longer part of Incoterms® 2010. If using marine terms, the contract or purchase order must exactly state what "on board the vessel" means for the transaction—where the container is on the vessel and the item to be placed.

11.4.2.3 Cost and Freight (CRF) + Named Place (Port on Buyer's Side)

- Delivery – seller delivers goods packaged for shipment on board the seller-designated vessel at the port on the seller's side
- Seller handles pre-carriage and main carriage
- Buyer handles on-carriage following delivery to port on buyer's side
- Risk passes from seller to buyer once goods are on board the vessel
- Insurance – neither party is required to insure goods
- Export clearance – handled by seller
- Import clearance – buyer is responsible for the customs requirements and associated costs (fees, duties, etc.)

Note: Even though risk passes from seller to buyer on the seller's side (once loaded per contract), seller contracts for and pays freight necessary to bring goods to the named port on the buyer's side.

11.4.2.4 Cost Insurance Freight (CIF) + Named Place (Port on Buyer's Side)

- Delivery – seller delivers goods packaged for shipment on board the seller-designated vessel at the port on seller's side
- Seller handles pre-carriage and main carriage
- Buyer handles on-carriage following delivery to port on the buyer's side
- Risk passes from seller to buyer once goods are on board the vessel
- Insurance – seller is required to procure minimum coverage against buyer's risk of loss or damage to the goods during carriage
- Export clearance – handled by seller
- Import clearance – buyer is responsible for the customs requirements and associated costs (fees, duties, etc.)

Note: Even though risk passes from seller to buyer on the seller's side (once loaded per contract), the seller contracts for and pays freight necessary to bring goods to the named port on the buyer's side, same as CPT + insurance coverage.

11.5 How to Use the Incoterms® 2010 Rules

Incoterms® rules do say which party in the sales contract has the obligation to make carriage or insurance arrangements, when the seller delivers the goods to the buyer, and which costs each party is responsible for. Incoterms® rules, however, say nothing about the price to be paid or the method of its payment. Neither do they deal with the transfer of ownership of the goods, or the consequences of a breach of contract. These matters are normally dealt with through express terms in the contract of sale or in the law governing that contract. The parties should be aware that mandatory local law may override any aspect of the sale contract, including the chosen Incoterms® rule.

References

Fisher, R., & Ury, W. (2012). *Getting to yes: Negotiating an agreement without giving in.* New York, NY: Random House Business Books.

Menard, R. (2004). *You're the buyer: You negotiate it!* Bloomington, IN: Author House.

About the Author

 **AJAY BHARGOVE** has successfully procured multimillion-dollar projects within power distribution utility services—solar, oil, and gas—as well as combined-cycle power-plant industries. His most recent engagements include volunteering for the PMI North India Chapter as an author and reviewer of various articles.

He has been leading a commercial and procurement organization for the service sector with a multinational company in Gurgaon, India.

He has more than a decade of diverse experience in the power and energy industry. He is a self-motivated individual and believes in giving back to the community. He has given volunteer training on project procurement for candidates preparing for the Project Management Professional (PMP)® certification exam. He is also known for his contribution within organizations for making teams aware of Incoterms® 2010 and other procurement and commercial-related training.

He is an active member of the Project Management Institute (PMI) and is the author of several popular articles for his local chapter, including:

- Pros and Cons of Negotiation
- Project Risks and Procurement
- How to Deal with Project Changes and Succeed

Apart from his association with PMI, he is an active associate member of the Institution of Engineers (India). He is also an OHSAS 18001:2007 Lead Auditor from DNV-AS. He holds a bachelor's degree in electrical engineering with honors from Chottu Ram State College of Engineering (Murthal), Sonepat (Haryana).

He has received multiple written appreciations for his negotiation strategies and substantial savings to the organizations he has worked for.

Above all, he is a proud son, husband, and father of two beautiful children, Aarav and Ahana.